Invisible Machine Appliqué and Beyond

Dawn Cameron-Dick

To Christine —
Have happy days
Stitching with IMA !

Cheers —

2016

'The Lyfe so short ...
the craft so long to learne'

TEAMWORK
CRAFTBOOKS

ISBN 0 9532590 6 4
British Library Cataloguing in Publication Data
A catalogue record for this book is available from the British Library

Designed and edited by Christopher and Gail Lawther, Teamwork Craftbooks,
44 Rectory Walk, Sompting, Lancing, West Sussex BN15 0DU

Printed by Dualcrest Printers
3 The Parade, Cokeham Road, Lancing, West Sussex

CONTENTS

What teacher wouldn't revel to hear comments like: 'I never thought I could do this!', 'It really is so easy!', 'I'd left that quilt unfinished for years until I learned IMA, and then I finished the top in a week!' and 'Who'd have thought my wee machine was so clever!?'

BEFORE WE BEGIN I'd like to introduce myself to those of you who are trying IMA for the first time, and also provide an update for my established IMA friends.

♥ Having lived in a rambling Grade 2 listed home in Tunbridge Wells, Kent for six years, our family dynamics changed, and in 2002 I moved to a stone barn conversion outside the lovely Midlands town of Stamford. It's more of a studio with a house attached so it suits me just perfectly!

♥ My parents Frank & Lorraine Sobczak, who lived with us in Kent, felt that Florida better suited their sun-starved bones, so they've now relocated to Fort Myers, Florida.

♥ My husband Gordon left his position in Nigeria and moved to Accra, Ghana where he is much happier and certainly more appreciated by the lovely people there.

It seems that in Africa, even the bakers appliqué!

♥ Eldest son Christopher and wife Renee have produced two grandchildren, Sierra Dawn and Mason, in addition to Renee's son Andrew. They have settled in Colorado and are still waiting for the Double Wedding Ring quilt I promised them at their wedding in 1996!

HELLO! Welcome ...

to the wonderful world of IMA. To those of you who have read my first book, *Invisible Machine Appliqué*, I hope you've been well and truly bitten by the IMA bug and that you're anxious to learn more and see what else this great technique has to offer. If you're new to the IMA scene may I tell you how pleased I am that you've decided to give Invisible Machine Appliqué a try! I promise to do my best to entertain and empower you in this book. After all, what is education but power?

The more you know, the more you're capable of!

I must admit to being absolutely flabbergasted by the overwhelming response to IMA ever since the first book came out. Quilters everywhere have shown boundless enthusiasm and satisfaction in its simple concept. Every class I have taught has assured me that there was a definite need for an easy, effective way to produce the look of hand-done appliqué on your sewing machine.

♥ Eldest daughter Hollis now has a wee daughter, Anastasia. They are in Colorado at the moment but are still determined to follow a dream to settle in Australia. Hollis made little A an IMA quilt before she was born and now we're working trans-Atlantic on another.

Hollis' quilt for Anastasia

♥ Rachel is currently in her 4th year reading Classics at Edinburgh University. She joined the TA and is contemplating a military career. Another victim of the travel bug, she assisted me teaching in Cape Town, became PADI certified in Egypt, learnt to sky dive in Germany and took part in a month-long Uni exchange in Greece!

♥ My youngest son Alastair, the last to flee the nest, is at University in Leicester. He and his partner Emma had a boy named Roman (after Aunt Helen's husband!) in February 2004. Study, work and baby fill most of his time now.

Was it something I said?

So with a smaller house, tiny garden and a larger studio I have more time to teach and travel. Now I intend to sew and challenge myself as never before ... not only with IMA, but in all aspects of quilting, which has been my life-blood for over 30 years.

The quilting world has provided me with opportunities and accomplishments I never dreamed possible. It has introduced me to people who have enriched my life and who have, I am certain, taught me more than I have ever taught them.

It seems that everyone you meet in this industry is a potential friend. Quilters always welcome you with open arms, hearts and minds!

Quilting can be very personal. Every quilt I've made has a story or meaning attached to it, so throughout the book you'll be introduced to various family members and hear the stories behind the making of each quilt.

Perhaps this is all a bit personal, but I want to share it with you because I know we all have similar stories and I hope you'll be able to relate to mine. I've also 'decorated' the pages with photographs of places here in England that are special to me, and I hope that they'll make you smile.

IMA and Beyond was originally introduced at the end of my last book as *Innovations In IMA*, but as the book took shape it developed a mind of its own so ' ... and Beyond' seemed much more appropriate.

I've never thought of myself as an artist, or a particularly clever person. I'm just an idea farmer ... in other words a teacher – a guide. My goal is to give you the information you need, provide you with a firm kick in the bum, and send you off to create.

So, what are we waiting for?

Let's go IMA-ing*!

And remember ...

The mind is like a parachute ...

it only functions when it's open.

* I'll use the term IMA to describe the technique throughout the book. For example: 'No, I cannot feed your rabbit ... I'm IMAing!', 'I think I'll IMA this' or 'Yes, indeed this has been IMAed'. Look for the word soon in your *Oxford English Dictionary* ...

Updates on machines, threads and needles

A good machine should be easy enough for anyone to use ...

Sewing machine update

In the first chapter of Book One I spoke about choosing a sewing machine. As with all things, machines continue to change, so I'll try to get you up to date on what's available today.

New models appear on a regular basis, with most of them boasting names such as 'Quilters' Choice' or 'Quilters' Dream,' suggesting that somehow very talented quilters were involved in the creation of that particular machine. So, if you want to be as wonderful as these quilters you certainly must buy this machine. In most cases nothing could be further from the truth. What *is* true is that quilters buy the majority of sewing machines today, and all the manufacturers are vying for your money. Everyone wants a piece of the Quilting Pie! So buyers must be on their toes.

> all stitches are fully adjustable
> feed dogs that drop
> does blind hem stitch
> dial controls
> large stitching platform
> can stop with needle down
> *Other Handy Features:*
> leg lift
> open-toe appliqué foot

I feel that it's getting harder and harder to find a robust, reliable, easy-to-control sewing machine that truly meets a quilter's basic needs. May I remind you of what those needs are?

- Total adjustability of width and length on all stitches, dials being preferable to buttons which only give you width choices in steps (ie 1, 1.5, 2, 2.5 etc).

- Feed dogs that drop easily.

- A good-size sewing platform or table to support our quilts.

- The ability to stop in the needle down position (invaluable when quilting, or doing appliqué or embroidery).

- Good lighting.

- Easy, accessible tension adjustments on both the top thread and the bobbin.

Then, of course, I would add a blind hem stitch, an open-toe embroidery foot, a front-loading bobbin and a knee lift to my personal list of needs.

To me this doesn't seem like too much to ask – but just try to find one machine that does it all. I know of several machines (no longer made) that **do** do it all, but that was then and this is now! So what are we to do?

Often in classes students apologise for their machine's limitations by saying, 'I just wanted something simple,' or 'It was all I could afford.' The best machine should be simple to use and generally affordable for most budgets. We do not want to pay for flash or clever gadgets, but that is what we often get.

I probably see over a hundred machines a month in my workshops, and the same problems keep coming up. Read over my list below and see if you don't suffer from some of the same frustrations as countless other quilters. It may not solve your problem, but at least you won't feel alone!

- Very expensive machines that simply will not allow you to adjust the width and length on every stitch – but which you can set to embroider Mickey Mouse playing tennis while you wash the windows! So very useful …

- Machines with pitifully small sewing platforms, or models that require you to buy an extension table to sew successfully.

- Machines which make it difficult, if not impossible, for you to adjust bobbin tensions. Quilters are creative people, and we need to be able to play with our threads!

- Machines with buttons that only allow you specific lengths or widths. What do you do if 1.5 is too small but 2 is too large?

Over the past years I've compiled an 'IMA Bad Boy' list, consisting of machines that constantly let my quilters down. If you think you may have an IMA Bad Boy, you can check out the list on my website (www.morningstarquilts.com), which is updated regularly. Please feel free to contact me with the details of your particular Bad Boy, which I can share with others. Also, if you have a truly remarkable machine please let me know about that one as well, so that I can spread the word!

In the interim, if you're already in possession of an IMA Bad Boy I'd like to offer some general suggestions on how you might override your machine's limitations:

- Sometimes the official blind hem stitch won't reduce enough, but if your machine has a backwards blind hem facility sometimes, oddly enough, this one will reduce! If your machine bites to the right and you find it cumbersome to sew with your appliqué under the machine, look to see if your machine has a pattern reverse button. It may look something like one of these:

   If you activate this button it will flip the stitch over to a left-hand bite, and you're sorted.

- Try looking for another stitch similar to the blind hem – for example the buttonhole or appliqué stitch (see page 8). You may be able to adjust this stitch. If it stitches in the wrong direction, refer to the previous suggestion …

- Activate your twin needle protector button, if you have one. Of course we both know that you will still actually be sewing with only one needle, but you've fooled the machine into thinking it has two, and so it will automatically cut every stitch width in half! Just what we wanted. (It's a bit like dealing with kids!) Now you'll have to increase the stitch width because the 2 width that was too wide has now become a 1 width that will be too narrow. The 3 width may work: give it a try.

Unfortunately, some machines with a twin needle button won't allow it to activate on the blind hem stitch because it thinks that you'd never really want to do a hem with a twin needle … ARRGH! Who wants a machine with an opinion anyway … it should just follow orders!

- If all else fails you may have to resort to a long, narrow zigzag (see page 8).

If you're currently in the market for a new machine, why not read the chapter on buying sewing machines in _Invisible Machine Appliqué_? It may help you avoid making a costly mistake.

Stitch update

In the spotlight today :

The blind hem stitch!

The original, and still the best, choice for most applications. Let's hear it for him, gals!

Made up of a few straight stitches and an ever-so-cute little 'bite' stitch that jumps to the left and grabs hold of our appliqué. When teamed up with a top-quality invisible thread it produces a superb, hand-done looking appliqué. Don't you just love it?

BUT …

There is another contender:

Please let me introduce the buttonhole or appliqué stitch.

A nice little stitch similar to the blind hem, as it also provides a few straight stitches but then deviates by giving you a straight 'bite' stitch rather than a little peak. Very neat and tidy. Not all machines have this stitch but it is becoming more popular: Bernina, Viking and some models of Janome have it at the moment. A stitch well worth trying even if you have a blind hem!

Beware: be sure not to use the stitch that looks like the buttonhole stitch in the drawing but actually stitches back on itself between bites:

It's best to test the stitch on scrap fabric first.

AND …

If you have none of these or cannot adjust the stitches you have, there is always:

The long, soft zigzag.

Not a satin stitch, mind you, but a soft, gentle stitch that zigs on the background fabric and zags over onto the appliqué edge. Try various different widths and lengths until you get something that resembles this:

It won't be quite as invisible as the blind hem or buttonhole stitch, but it's better than a poke in the eye with a sharp stick, and you will be able to produce pretty decent appliqué!

Needle update

Over 15 years of teaching, and the response to the needle information in Book One, have definitely shown me that the machine piecers and quilters of today have become a much more demanding and sophisticated bunch of ladies! In class they sit enthralled as I explain about needle types, sizes and abilities. They furiously scribble notes, and when I finish they practically rend their garments and lament 'Why hasn't anyone ever told me this?' Why indeed …

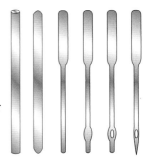

The simple answer is that the needle manufacturers themselves do very little to explain their product to their customers. I guess they just expect us to be born knowing why an Embroidery Needle is different from a Top Stitch Needle. Maybe I was deprived, but it certainly wasn't covered in any of my schools.

So, to expand on the basic information in Book One, I offer you the following information:

a sewing machine needle passes through nearly 30 stages of production. These include: straightening and cutting the original wire; grinding the ends; swaging (forging to the correct length); stamping and punching the eye out (sounds like a fight outside a pub); marking the needle with the correct details; milling the groove; flash-grinding and adding the point; hardening; scraping; straightening; polishing; and electroplating.

And all of this just to give you the perfect tool for every thread and fabric you could sew.

Types of needle

The number of the needles used on almost all domestic sewing machines made today is **130/705**. After this number is usually a letter **H**, which stands for *hohlkehle*; this is the German word for scarf, and describes the shape of needle needed for domestic sewing machines.

Also, the Schmetz people now colour-code many of their needles, so if you use this brand you won't have to use the nail varnish technique mentioned in Book One! Their colour codes and letters are as follows:

H-Q = Quilting Needle   has a green band

H-J = Denim/Jeans   has a blue band
(think of blue jeans and it'll be easy to remember!)

H-M = Microtex Sharps   has a purple band

H-E = Embroidery has a red band

H-MET = Metallic has a gold band

Always buy the best you can afford: with needles you really do get what you pay for.

When you're replacing a needle, be sure the flat side is to the back (for all modern domestic machines) and that the needle is pushed totally up into the machine. Tighten the screw and sew a few stitches on scrap fabric to be sure that all is well before going on to your project.

When do I need to change my needle?

It's difficult to suggest a particularly helpful answer to this question. Every 1000 metres of thread? Who keeps an eye on that!? Every ten hours of sewing? Same answer. How about … OFTEN! Unfortunately, needles never look old and in need of replacing (we should be so lucky), but just think of all that's happening to them:

- They get nicks on the point from sewing over pins.

- They get dull from many hours of sewing (polyester wadding dulls needles very quickly).

- The eye itself erodes as the thread passes through it thousands of times a minute.

- The needle bends every time we pull our threads out before cutting them.

So you see, eventually you will need to replace your old friend. Put him out to pasture (so to speak).

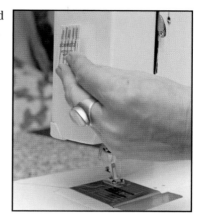

While sewing, I find it extremely useful to stick my needle package to the head of my machine with reusable tacking gum. This way I know what needle is currently in my machine and I know what packet it came from.

When returning a partially-used needle to the plastic packaging I put it in backwards – that is, with the flat edge to the front (they come with the rounded edge front when you buy them!) This way, the next time I take the package out I know that that needle has already been used, and I will then throw it away when I've finished sewing.

Finally, remember to use the smallest needle you can get your thread through. 70/10 and 80/12 are probably the best sizes for our piecing and appliqué. I love the Denim/Jeans needle, but the Microtex Sharps are also very good. I buy one-size-only packages to save on waste, and when in doubt I chuck it out.

Share this information with everyone you know. That way you won't have to listen to them gripe because things have gone pear-shaped. They just won't! Correct needles make such a difference.

A quick word about pins …

Now that you're oh-so-clever about needles, please give some thought to your choice of pins. Most students are sewing with pins that could substitute as nails! We need fine, long pins such as silk pins. Look for a top-quality pin that is about 0.5mm diameter and about 1¼in long. Avoid those huge, plastic-headed pins that melt the moment an iron touches them. There is a lovely type of pin available now with a no-melt head. Heaven!

Fine pins create less distortion of the fabric during pinning and so will increase your accuracy. They say a bad workman blames his tools … in this case it's a valid comment. So throw out that mess of mismatched pins you inherited from Mrs Noah, and invest in some lovely new ones. Please!

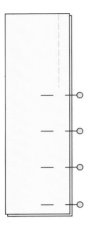

And while we're on the subject of pins, try always to pin perpendicular to the raw edge of your pieces. Be sure that the heads are off the fabric to the right and it will be very easy for you to remove them just before the machine needle gets there. Although it is possible, it's safer not to sew over pins.

So many threads, so little time

Let's talk a bit about threads. This may sound about as exciting as watching paint dry, but threads are a vital part of a quilt's success. Thread is what holds all your wonderful ideas and expensive, carefully-chosen fabrics together. And it's what will determine whether in 100 years your quilt will still be in one piece and admired, or just a heap of frayed bits in a trash heap. Was that too harsh? Sorry, but I feel so strongly about this that I must lecture.

Pause for a moment and think about it …

Our quilts are our immortality. Something made with our hands and our hearts; and no matter how simple or crudely made, they were made with love and are a reflection of ourselves. I don't have the time or manpower to build a pyramid, but if I choose the best fabrics and threads for my quilts I stand a pretty good chance of them being around in hundreds of years when I am dust.

They might still make someone smile or encourage them to make a quilt themselves, and in that small way I live on. And so will you. Our quilts deserve the very best we can give them so **please do not scrimp**.

Buy the very best quality thread you can afford!

There are basically two types of thread: **utility** and **decorative**.

UTILITY THREADS

Utility threads hold things together with the minimum of fuss; they are our unsung heroes. For most quilting projects the thread should be:

Top-quality 100% cotton, 50/3 or 40/2 weight, thread.

I only use neutral or medium-grey thread depending on whether the majority of my fabric is light or dark. I never use black as it disintegrates too quickly, and coloured threads are just not practical as we have so many different colours in our work.

As with needles, you definitely get what you pay for when buying thread. In my opinion some of the best threads currently available are:

- YLI Select (40/2)
- Mettler (50/3)
- DMC Machine Embroidery (50/2) and
- Madeira Tanne (50/3).

Note: *the numbers after the thread names refer to their weight and ply. I could explain how it all works in vivid detail, but I know I'd have you asleep in 3.5 seconds! Suffice to say; the **larger** the number, the **finer** the thread. But this too can be confusing, as that would imply that the YLI thread is far too heavy – but that's without taking the ply into account.*

Although thread people will probably shudder at this, I've found an easy way to decipher it all: simply divide the ply into the weight. For example, here are the threads listed above from thickest to thinnest:

- Mettler and Madeira are 50 weight ÷ by 3 ply = number 16.5-ish

- YLI is 40 weight ÷ by 2 ply = number 20

- DMC is 50 weight ÷ by 2 ply = number 25 (the finest)

Find one you like. Buy several spools, then go home and fill half a dozen bobbins with your new thread; this way you'll have a bobbin ready the minute your previous one empties. Always fill bobbins from empty and try not to fill them too fast – this could stretch your threads and make them more prone to snap.

With invisible thread I always use a 60/2 ply thread in the bobbin. 60/2 is even finer than 50/3. (Remember the formula? The weight 60 ÷ by the ply 2 = number 30. And the larger the number the finer the thread … By Jove, you've got it! Who's the clever bunny then!?)

I use either neutral or grey depending on my background fabric. YLI and Mettler both make a lovely 60/2 thread which is also wonderful to piece with. I don't like 'bobbin fill' threads as they are usually polyester, and I feel that this creates too strong a stitch with the nylon invisible thread. 50/3 is also fine in the bobbin, but you may have to reduce your upper tension (or tighten the bobbin) when using it to avoid the thread showing on the top.

What about polyester threads?
And now *once again* a word about The Polyester Issue …

I explained my feeling about using polyester thread in quilts in Book One, but I think another mention here wouldn't go amiss!

There are two simple rules for choosing threads:

- Your thread should match your fabric. Natural threads for natural fabrics, and synthetic threads for synthetic fabrics.

- Your thread should always be equal (in strength) to, or weaker than, the fabric it is sewing.

I know that polyester is cheaper and is easily available. And it is a great thread for the use it was intended for … sewing synthetic fabric! Most quilts are 100% cotton and we need a thread that will break before it cuts through our fabric. Our quilts are under constant stress (sound familiar?) We handle them, sleep under them, wash and fold them. At some point a seam will be pulled and one of two things can happen. The thread can break, or the thread holds and cuts through the seam. I can re-sew a broken thread, but I cannot repair a seam that has been cut.

Polyester has tiny, abrasive edges that work like saw blades against our cotton fibres, and over time they'll cut through the seam. Below is the first quilt I made, in 1971 (OK, I can hear you laughing! Remember it *was* my first!): many of the seams are cut.

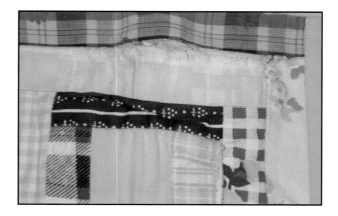

Polyester also shrinks with heat when we iron, and it creates more static when it's running through the sewing machine, and this can adversely affect the stitch formation.

Convinced yet? I hope so. Please put a marker in the book on this page and then run, don't walk, to your quilting basket and remove any and all polyester threads. Use them only for what they were intended. The same goes for cotton-coated polyester: it's a wolf in sheep's clothing. In a very short time the cotton fluff they coat the poly with rubs off, and you have the Big Bad Wolf all over your quilt. Don't fall for it. Stick with cotton … please! **Remember, you deserve the best**.

DECORATIVE THREADS

Silks, rayons, metallics and polyester sparklies all fall into this category. They are the pretty boys: they sit up front and centre stage as accents on appliqué or as quilting threads. I have even taken to trying stitching 'Not-Quite-Invisible Machine Appliqué' (see page 48) with some of them. Great fun! Just keep in mind their limitations. For example:

Silk thread

Lovely and strong to sew with. I prefer Japanese silk as they boil the cocoons to get the thread out, whereas the Chinese cut the cocoon open and sometimes this cuts the silk filaments. A wonderful soft thread to quilt with, silk is also unsurpassed for hand appliqué. It slides through the fabric and virtually disappears into the edge of the appliqué!

If you're stitching by hand use a milliners size 10 needle. On the machine use a 70/10 Denim/Jeans or a Microtex Sharp with a 60/2 cotton in the bobbin.

Rayon

Made from wood shavings. No, really! Very popular for satin stitch appliqué. It often comes in two weights: 30 weight, which is thicker, and 40 weight which is a larger number and so … is thinner! YLI has an acrylic 40wt thread called Ultrasheen, which is a rayon alternative and is excellent for satin stitch.

I wouldn't use these threads for extensive quilting on quilts that will get heavy use, as the rayon weakens with continued exposure to water. But they are great for wall-hangings and garment embellishment. Use a 75/11 Embroidery needle or a Quilting needle on the machine with cotton in the bobbin.

Metallics

A common complaint among students is that metallic threads are difficult to sew with. Breaking. Fraying. Skipping stitches. And no wonder.

Metal cannot be spun like cotton, so it's usually made by wrapping fine strips of the metal around an invisible thread. Both are slippery, and so with extensive machine sewing it's bound to strip.

A few tips for metallic success:

- sew slower
- lower top tension
- put 60/2 cotton thread in the bobbin
- put a line of Sewer's Aid on the spool of thread to lubricate and cut down on static and heat build-up.

When stitching with metallic threads always use an 80/12 Metallic or 90/14 Embroidery needle. These have a deeper cut at the back, which means that the fabric will take longer to cling to the needle. This allows your machine more time to form a stitch. Also the eye of the needle is wider and has an oblong shape; this allows the metallic thread to pass through more easily, and prevents the eye of the needle from closing in on the thread as it heats up from excessive stitching.

Unusual decorative threads

There are so many of these threads about that it's impossible for me to cover them all. Usually an embroidery needle works well, in the smallest size you can thread. Use cotton in the bobbin, sew a sample piece first and if there is breakage try Sewer's Aid. If it just won't sew, perhaps it would be happier in your bobbin.

Bobbin talk

Sometimes people get confused about which way the bobbin should be put into the machine. An easy tip is to think of the bobbin itself as a clock …

If it is a front-loading bobbin, put it in the case and pull the thread gently. The bobbin itself should turn in a **clockwise** fashion (a).

 If you have a drop-in bobbin, place it in the machine and gently pull the thread. The bobbin this time should turn ***anti-clockwise*** or ***counter-clockwise*** (**b**).

Also always thread your machine with the ***foot up***; this opens the tension discs to accept the thread. These discs close when the foot is put down to sew.

... and tension talk

Getting a perfect balance between your top thread and your bobbin thread is quite aptly called 'tension.' Just the suggestion to 'adjust your tension ... ' makes most quilters break into a cold sweat! In reality there's no need to do so. A balanced tension is simply having your two threads meeting in the centre of two pieces of fabric (**c**).

c   top fabric   top thread
bottom fabric   bobbin thread

Why not try this simple test of your machine's tension? Thread your machine with a coloured thread on the top and a neutral thread of the same make and weight in the bobbin. Cut two strips of fabric (colours don't matter here) and press them together. Now sew a seam about 4in long and remove the piecing from your machine. If the top coloured thread shows on the bottom, as in **d**, either the top thread is too loose or the bobbin thread too tight.

d   top fabric
bottom fabric   top thread
                       bobbin thread
top thread too loose

Turn the upper tension dial to a higher number (**e**) or loosen the screw on the bobbin by turning it to the left ¼ turn (**f**).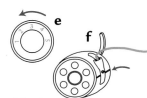

Now sew another 4in seam and look again. If the neutral bobbin thread shows on the top, as here (**g**), then either the top tension is too tight or the bobbin tension is too loose.

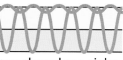

g   top fabric   top thread
bottom fabric   bobbin thread
top thread too tight

Turn the upper tension dial to a lower number (**h**) or tighten the screw on the bobbin by turning it to the right ¼ turn (**i**).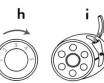

Without sewing you can easily test your bobbin tension by holding the thread and letting the bobbin case hang loose (**j**). If it drops swiftly to the floor your tension is too loose. Tighten the screw to the right.

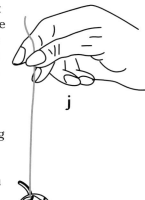

If it doesn't move at all (go ahead, give it a yank as if you were playing with a yoyo), then your tension could be too tight. Before making any adjustments I suggest that you do the sewing test above. Every machine is different and your machine may just be a bit 'uptight'!

Always think of the bobbin screw as a clock.

Turn the screw only 1-2 'hours' at a time, and always make note of where it was when you started.

These suggestions are for front-loading bobbins; if your machine has a drop-in bobbin, please check your manual.

You may find you need various different tensions for different weights or decorative threads. Polyester tends to drag more than cotton thread, and thus needs a slightly looser tension. The same applies to invisible threads.

If you find yourself changing bobbin tensions often, you may benefit from buying an additional bobbin case. Since this is mainly for 'fancy' threads I mark mine with a bit of nail varnish (below); it looks posh, so reminds me that it's the one I leave loose for fancy threads.

Some Common-Sense Advice On Wadding/Batting

So much choice ... so little information! That seems to be the big problem when it comes to choosing your wadding (or batting, as it's called in America). And making the right choice can make such a difference to the finished look and longevity of your quilt. Whenever I give a talk and show my quilts, one of the first questions most people ask is 'What wadding do you use?' I am a fanatical hand quilter, but I also machine quilt, so I like my wadding to be easy to needle and not too thick. This way I can use both techniques and not have a problem. But please remember:

No one wadding is ideal for every quilter or for every quilt!

You must give almost as much consideration to what's inside your quilt as you do to the fabric on the outside. I don't wish to spend pages and pages describing different brands of wadding, as the list seems to change daily, but what I do want to do is tell you something about the different types of waddings available and let you make your own best-educated decision.

Types of wadding

Cotton waddings

 Cotton is breathable (thus it's cooler in the summer).

It does not melt (safer for baby quilts).

There is the perception that cotton wadding and cotton fabrics are more 'traditional.'

The wadding can also shrink slightly, to give a quilt an antique look.

Cotton 'clings' to the quilt top, and does not shift as much as some other waddings when machine quilting.

✗ Most cottons are harder to needle when hand quilting; this can create larger stitches, and also slows you down.

Cotton's natural shrinkage can be a problem when it isn't part of the design.

Cotton requires closer quilting, so it takes longer to make a piece if you're quilting by hand.

Some brands contain seeds or bits of seed which can deflect the needle, or burst and leave oil stains on a light-coloured quilt top.

Bleached cotton is available for use with light quilt tops, but the bleaching process can dry out the fibres and make hand quilting drag even more.

Polyester waddings

 Polyester is easily available.

It comes in a variety of weights.

It's inexpensive, easy to wash and quick to dry.

Polyester will allow more space between stitches, has more loft, and will not shrink.

 Polyester can be too warm in the summer.

It can melt if ironed or exposed to flame.

Some brands tend to beard. (Bearding is when loose fibres pull through to the top of the quilt and appear as fuzz or fine hairs!)

Polyester can stretch (especially lengthways), and so may not be a good choice for wall quilts. Polyester can be more difficult to machine quilt due to its bulk. (Thin polyester waddings machine quilt just fine.)

Poly/cotton waddings

This type of wadding is usually made as an 80% cotton/20% polyester blend in an effort to provide the best of both worlds.

 You get the traditional look and feel of cotton wadding, but the polyester makes it easier to needle and allows you to stitch farther apart.

 Some brands of poly/cotton feel very coarse. It may be hard to disregard this, and to remember that the wadding will be sandwiched *inside* the quilt! Finished, it feels just like 100% cotton.

Wool waddings

Wool wadding is available as 100% wool (Hobbs), and as 60% wool/40% polyester (Matilda's Own)

 Wool is naturally flame-resistant (good for baby quilts).

It provides warmth and loft without being heavy.

Wool is naturally breathable (does not get overly hot or cold).

Wool has good drape and little or no shrinkage.

Wool absorbs up to 33% of its own weight in moisture without feeling damp (as opposed to 4% for synthetics). This makes it excellent for cold, damp climates …

But most importantly, wool is a dream come true for hand quilters! The needle just slides through the quilt like a hot knife through butter.

 Wool can be more expensive and harder to find than other waddings.

At one time there was a worry that the wool would attract pests, who would nibble up your quilt top on their way to the wool! But never fear: today they add an antibacterial solution to the wadding which deters those nasty wee bugs.

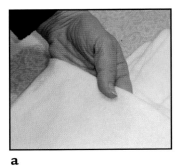

a

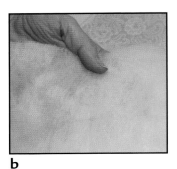

b

e

f

Here are two other terms you may see in reference to wadding:

needlepunched and *bonded*

- *Needlepunched wadding* (**a**) refers to a method where the wadding is passed through a machine that pierces it with hundreds of barbed needles, which tangle the fibres together as they are withdrawn. This process keeps the fibres together without the need for glues or resins … which makes it easier to needle. Hooray! You can also wash needlepunched wadding without the fear of bearding or separation. These waddings can be somewhat flat.

- *Bonded waddings* (**b**) are made of fluffy sheets of … well, fluff … which are resin-bonded to keep them together. You seldom get a bearding problem with quality bonded waddings, and they generally have more loft than needlepunched waddings.

So, how do I choose?

Well, there are several factors to consider:

- What look do you want your quilt to have?

Will it be a traditional quilt (**c**) with a flat, old-fashioned, 'used' look? Then use 100% cotton.

Or do you want a contemporary, fluffy quilt (**d**) for your bed? Use a medium-weight bonded polyester.

c

d

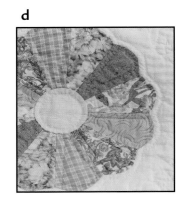

- What's the destination of your quilt?

Will you be making a quilt that is intended to hang on the wall (**e**) ? If so, try a needlepunched wadding.

Or will it be a snuggle quilt for the sofa (**f**), which you'll then want to be soft, with a nice drape? Lightweight bonded polyester would be best.

- Other considerations

Do you enjoy hours of hand quilting? Then try a wool wadding (**g**)!

Does the fibre content really matter to you? Are you a purist who says, 'Only cotton in my cotton quilt?' Are there allergies in the family? Is the quilt meant to keep you extra-warm, or is it for the summer?

How much time are you willing to spend on the quilting stage? Will it be hand- or machine-quilted? Or both?

I always feel it's worth the effort to make a few sample squares any time you try a new wadding. Maybe you could talk your quilt group into doing a project where everyone makes and labels a 12in square that has been half hand-

g

and half machine-quilted. Wash them when finished and label them with details of the wadding you used. It would also be helpful if half the piece was light and half was dark. Keep these in a box and add to the samples as new waddings become available. It's an easy project and will prove invaluable in avoiding costly (to your sanity!) wadding nightmares.

When you do find wadding you like, stick to it! I have religiously used the same polyester wadding (Mountain Mist Quilt-Light) since the mid 70s because it works for me. I know how it needles. I know it washes beautifully. I know it doesn't beard, because some of my quilts are nearly 30 years old and they've stood the test of time (far better than me, I regret!).

You might even like to note which wadding you used on the label you make for the back of your quilt.

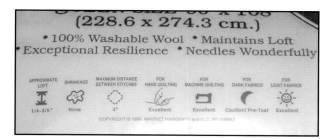

When it comes to piecing waddings I'm about as fond of that idea as I am about butchering my own meat! Why do it when bed-sized waddings can easily be bought in a package without all that effort? I buy my waddings in packs cut to the standard bed sizes. And the most important thing is that I get a package with all sorts of lovely words on it! The packaging should have lots of information for me. It should advise me on how far apart I can safely quilt. It should give me the fibre content of the wadding, and tell me if it's bonded or needlepunched. Then I can make an educated choice.

If you do buy wadding on a roll, the best ones will come with a paper band that has all this information on it. Make sure you ask the shop to give you a length of this; take it home and read it!

Sometimes the waddings come out of the packaging in a very wrinkled state. If you have the time, unroll the wadding and lay it out across a spare bed for a day to relax. Or if you're pressed for time, put the wadding in the tumble dryer on a very low temperature (or just on 'air dry') for about 5-10 minutes. You could also go over it with your hair dryer, but always keep your hand between the hot air and your wadding!

Bearding can be substantially reduced if you use tightly-woven (high thread count) fabrics, new top-quality needles and a quality 100% cotton thread. Polyester fabrics and thread encourage bearding. Don't use them! Oops, did that sound bossy? How about, 'Please don't ever, ever use polyester fabrics or thread in your quilts?' (See the thread update section on page 11 for the gory details!)

One final point ...

If you really **must** piece your wadding, don't even think of overlapping the seams or 'butting up' the straight edges. Harriet Hargreave (a respected American machine quilter) suggests making a serpentine line cut through the overlapped edges. Overlap your edges by about 6-8in, and then cut a wavy line through both layers at the same time (**a**).

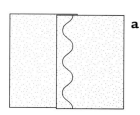

Remove the excess, plug one side into the other (**b**) and then hand tack the pieces together, using cotton thread and a ½in wide loose herringbone stitch (**c**).

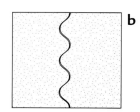

This way you will never get a ridge forming on your quilt from repeated folding, and there's virtually no chance of it pulling apart!

The Little-Known Art Of Blocking Quilts

Trees Please 1996

After quilting, but before binding, you might consider squaring up your quilt. Lots of lovely machine (or hand) quilting looks great, but it can distort the size and shape of your quilt. Densely-quilted sections can sometimes pucker, and those areas without much quilting can stretch.

When you're making a quilt, I'd advise you to cut your final border at least 1in wider than you need; this will allow you to trim a bit when you're squaring up the quilt.

In my quilt *Listen To The Leaves Singing* (see page 97) I had to do some serious work to get this heavily-quilted puppy to lay flat and square. It doesn't take terribly long – though it can be hard on the knees!

You will need:

- a metal tape measure
- a large plastic square ruler
- large, long yellow-headed pins
- and perhaps a sheet and an oscillating fan

1 Don't trim the backing or wadding before you begin blocking; simply pin the backing up and over the wadding and quilt top, and thread-tack it in place. This will protect the fragile edges of the wadding and fabric.

2 Wash your quilt per my instructions on page 23 – or, if you don't want to wash just yet, you can thoroughly wet the quilt. Either wet it in the bathtub (lay it on a large towel and give it a short spray with the shower nozzle), or put it on a gentle pre-wash cycle in your machine – just be sure it doesn't agitate or spin too aggressively.

3 Carefully remove the quilt: gently squeeze the excess moisture out.

4 Cover a carpeted floor with a large, clean, flat sheet; this will keep your quilt clean and help it to dry faster.

5 Open the quilt out onto the sheet, and remove the basting stitches holding the backing over the wadding.

6 It's best to use a metal tape measure at this stage – and have a friend at hand! Measure along each side and down the centre of the quilt (**a** and **b**). All these measurements should be the same. If they're not, ease or pull the offending edges until they're even. Repeat this for both the length and the width of the quilt. Use those long pins with the yellow heads and pin the quilt to the carpeted floor.

a

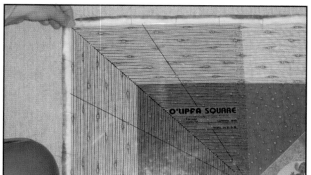

d

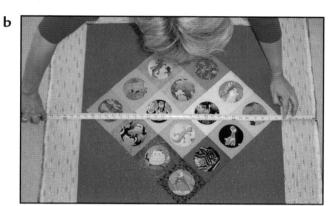

b

e

7 Now check the diagonal measurement (**c**): the corner-to-corner measurements must be identical if the quilt is to be square. Again, gently pull and coax to make the measurements match. Repin as necessary.

If you don't want to – or can't – completely wet the quilt, you can dampen it by spraying with a plant mister. Follow instructions 5-8, then use the steam button on your steam iron to set the quilt in shape (**f**) (remember though that you're *steaming* it, holding the iron a short distance away from the quilt's surface, not *pressing* it). You will still need to let it dry for several hours.

When the quilt is completely dry, unpin it and proceed with the binding.

c

8 Use your largest clear, plastic square and ensure that every corner is a right angle (**d**): trim with scissors if necessary.

9 Leave the quilt to dry. If it's in a high-traffic area, cover it with another sheet. I found that using a large fan oscillating over the quilt helped it to dry much faster (**e**).

f

My Favourite Binding Method

I have always used a straight-grain or double french fold binding. Some people insist that bias binding wears better, but I haven't found this to be true. Besides, it takes so much more fabric – and more time – to prepare. If you have curved edges on your quilt you will certainly need to make a bias binding, but for 99% of your quilts straight-edge binding works beautifully!

How much do I need?

First decide what **finished** width you want your binding to be. You'll need to cut your strips **six times** this width. For example, for your binding to finish up at ¾in you will need to cut 4½in strips across the grain on your fabric (that is, from selvedge edge to selvedge edge). You can generally assume that you can get 40in-long strips from each cut once the selvedge is removed.

So if your quilt is 90 x 106in you will calculate your binding needs as follows: (Please do not run away. This is NOT scary maths!)

$$90\text{in} \times 2 = 180\text{in}$$
$$106\text{in} \times 2 = 212\text{in}$$
$$\overline{392\text{in}}$$

Total length around quilt is then 392in.

$$392 \div 40^* = 9.8 \text{ strips}$$

(*40 is the length you can get across the fabric)

Rounded up: you'll need 10 strips.

Then you need to allow 2 strips for beginning, ending and turning mitred corners.

So I would cut 12 crossgrain strips, 4½in wide.

$$12 \times 4.5 \text{ width} = 54$$

Therefore, you'll need 54in, or 1½yd, of fabric to make your binding.

Preparing the binding

1 You will need to join the strips into one continuous strip. Place two strips, right sides together in a number 7 shape; offset the ends by about ¼in (**a**). Begin stitching in the top left-hand corner of the overlapped strips and sew to the bottom right-hand corner (**b**). Repeat with all the strips.

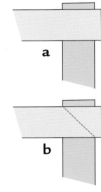

2 Trim the ends of the strips diagonally to ¼in beyond the seam and press the seams open (**c**). Press the entire bias strip in half along its length, **wrong sides together** (**d**).

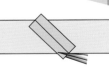

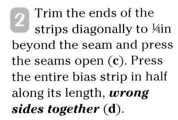

3 Open the beginning of the strip, fold the end of the strip over at a 45° angle and press (**e**).

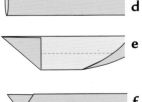

4 Refold the strip in half wrong sides together (**f**); your binding is now ready to be sewn on to the quilt.

Attaching the binding

1 Put the walking foot on your machine, and thread the machine with the same cotton thread in the top and bobbin. Activate the 'needle down' function if your machine has one; you'll find it very helpful. Don't trim the backing and wadding just yet: I do that after the binding is sewn on.

2 Position the binding on the front of the quilt half-way along one side, with the raw edges of the binding aligning with the raw edge of the border fabric (**a**). Pin the binding in place (or just hold it, if you're confident).

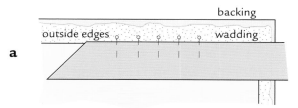

3 Begin stitching with a ¼in seam allowance, about 6in down from the tip of the folded binding (**b**). When you reach your first corner, stop sewing, with the needle in the machine, exactly ¼in from the edge of the quilt (**c**). I've found that stabbing a pin straight down through the folded binding directly into the quilt, exactly at the mitre, helps to guide me to the perfect spot to stop (with the needle down) and do the next quarter turn.

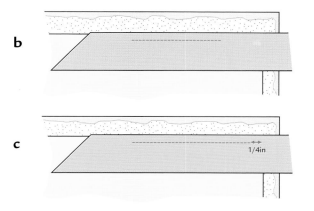

4 Turn the quilt a quarter turn anti-clockwise, then press and hold down the reverse button as you stitch backwards off the edge of the quilt (**d**).

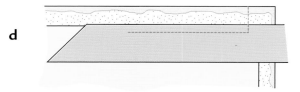

5 Raise the foot and pull the quilt towards you. Fold the binding back on top of itself, creating a 45° angle (**e**). Make a second fold by turning the binding back down on itself and lining it up with the second edge of the quilt (**f**).

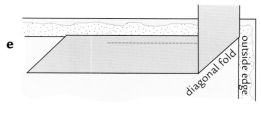

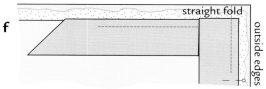

6 Lower the foot and sew down the next side. The first few stitches will be worked over the ones you made when you reversed off the quilt. Continue to the next corner and repeat from step 3. Carry on around the quilt.

7 When you near the end of the binding, insert the raw end of the binding strip into the folded edge (**g**) and sew them both as one.

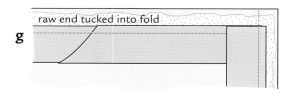

8 Trim away the excess backing and binding, allowing just a fine halo of both beyond the binding. This helps to fill out the binding, giving a more rounded look.

9 Now you can roll the folded edge of the binding to the back of the quilt and pin (**h**). At the corners, fold and mitre just as you did on the front.

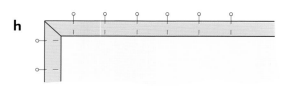

10 Hand stitch the folded edge to the back of the quilt with a blind hemstitch and a cotton thread that matches the binding fabric (**i**). Make sure that the folded edge of the binding covers the machine stitching lines, and don't let your blind hemming show through on the front of the quilt!

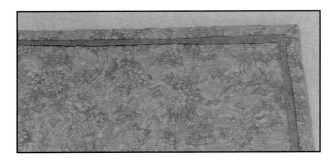

Now, isn't that a lovely sight to behold?

Food for thought ...

Sometimes it's nice to add just a hint of colour between the final border and the binding, by inserting a folded strip of fabric before you put the binding on. It's easy to do, and adds a special 'zing' to your quilt.

1 Cut enough 1in strips of contrasting fabric to make a strip long enough to go around your quilt edge. Add 12in for safety!

2 Fold this strip of fabric in half, wrong sides together (**a**).

3 Pin the strip onto the outside of the border with the raw edges matching (**b**); the fold will be towards the inside of the quilt top.

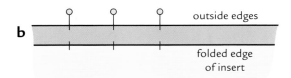

outside edges

folded edge
of insert

4 Stitch the strip to the border with a less-than-¼in seam allowance and a slightly longer stitch length (**c**); the longer stitch keeps the fabric from puckering.

5 At each corner, either form a mitre which will match the binding (**d**), or set them straight (**e**).

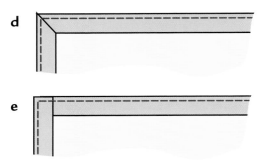

You could also 'stuff' this strip with a fine cotton cording (be sure that it's washable, and pre-wash it in hot water if you think it might shrink), or an acrylic 4-ply knitting yarn. Cotton will give a firmer look, and the acrylic a softer edge.

The only down side to this padded insert is that it makes sewing the binding on with a walking foot difficult. A zipper foot would be easier.

Steaming ahead

And finally, if you're pushed for time one day (who isn't?), and you just know you'll never get those miles of binding hand-sewn in time, try this quick fix.

After you've pressed your binding in half, place a strip of ¼in Steam-A-Seam2 ⅛in down from the folded edge and press in place. Once you've sewn the binding onto the front of the quilt, fold the folded edge over and press the binding to the back of the quilt. Voilà! It stays in place! Later, when the pressure is off, you can do the hand stitching – and it will be easy as there's no bonding agent within that first ⅛in. Any port in a storm ...

Washing Your Quilts

UNLESS you've made a purely decorative wall-hanging, every quilt will someday need to be washed. Washing does wonders for the final look of your quilt. It will not only remove airborne dirt, and oils deposited from your hands during the construction stage, but it also removes excess starch and finish from fabric which hasn't been pre-washed. And it will remove your pencil markings!

Depending on the 'heirloom-ability' of your quilt you can either wash it by hand, or in the machine. The instructions given below are intended for modern-day quilts made in the last 40 years or so. If you have an antique (pre 1950) quilt, I suggest that you seek professional help and advice on its care.

Please resist the temptation to send your lovely cotton quilt out to the dry cleaner's. The chemicals that they use are far too harsh, and they re-use the cleaning products so often that you're more likely to be putting dirt back into the quilt rather than taking it out. Just don't do it!

My bathtub method

1 Check for obvious stains (pre-treat them with stain remover), holes (repair them!) or loose threads (remove them).

2 Clean and rinse the bathtub, then fill it one third full with lukewarm water (80 to 85°F).

3 For washing you must use a gentle cleaner. Look for a product with the least number of ingredients: non-ionic and anionic detergents are best. You'll need a clear (no colourants added) washing product labelled 'non-ionic surfactant'; these wash best at low temperatures. Lauryl sodium sulphate is good and is known in America as Orvus Paste. Look for liquid, clear, hand-dishwashing products. Avoid hand-washing soaps meant for wool as they contain lanolin, and lanolin can settle on the fabric and actually attract dirt. It can also discolour light fabrics with extended use.

4 Gently lower the quilt into the water until it's completely submerged.

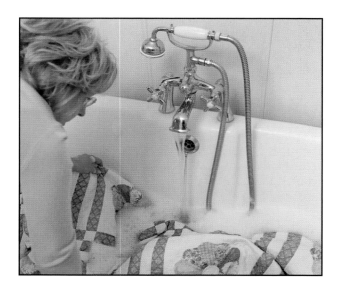

REMEMBER:
water can more than triple the weight of the quilt, and fibres weaken when wet, so BE GENTLE!

5 Sit beside the tub and keep an eye on that quilt! Much like you would a baby. Every once in a while gently move it about or agitate the water. Do not lift the quilt out of the water or squeeze it; the soap will do most of the cleaning. Leave it to soak for about 15-20 minutes. (Which is about how long anyone can sit beside a tub looking at wet fabric without going stark raving mad …)

6 Pull the plug and let the water drain. ***Don't touch the quilt***.

7 Replace the plug and refill the tub with the same temperature of water. Again, gently move the quilt around but don't lift it. This is rinsing number 1.

8 Drain the bathtub again and proceed with rinse 2. You may do a 3rd rinse if you feel it's necessary. A good test of whether you think the rinsing is complete, is to see if you'd be prepared to drink the water in the tub. You probably wouldn't want to if you really felt that there was any soap left in it!

9 Once the water has completely drained, carefully manoeuvre the quilt to one side of the tub and press it to push out as much water as possible. Then lay the largest bath towel you have alongside the quilt. Now pretend that you're a hospital aide, and ever-so-gently assist the quilt onto the towel. It's extremely useful to have an assistant at this stage, as they can support the soggy mess while you squeeze the towel to remove additional moisture.

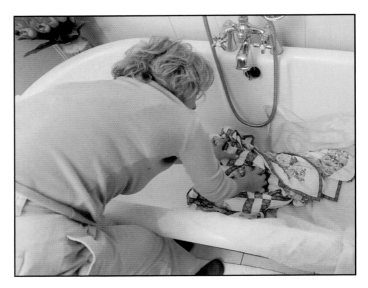

10 Using the towel as a sling, transport the 'patient' to the washing machine. Set the machine on the gentlest spin cycle, and only let it actually spin for one or two minutes.

11 You could then place the quilt into a tumble dryer and let it dry on LOW for no more than 10 minutes, but I prefer to use the grass. Just like in the old days, when they used drying fields or hedges to dry laundry, I feel that this is the best way to dry and freshen my quilts.

A few thoughts before you begin.

- If you have a live-in, or neighbourhood, four-legged friend, check for poop.

- Don't use the grass if it's been cut in the past 24 hours.

- And lastly, block off the afternoon for yourself because … the time-honoured tradition (little known in some areas) of Drying Quilts Outdoors can't be hurried.

The Definitive Art of Drying Quilts Outdoors

1 Lay the quilt face down on the grass and place a clean plate at each corner if it's at all windy.

2 If you're at odds with the local bird population (or are in fear of fading) you may lay a clean, white sheet over the quilt – but I'd rather have the sun on it.

3 Open up a lawn chair (preferably one with footrest and padding).

4 Prepare a pitcher of Pimms (with lots of fruit of course, so that it's good for you …) You may substitute home-made lemonade if you have North American tendencies.

5 Grab that new quilting book you've been dying to read (a quilt magazine will do at a pinch).

6 Position your body firmly in the chair. Place sun-hat on your head, sunscreen on your face, and proceed to watch the quilt dry. After about an hour (depending on the wind speed), flip the quilt over and quickly resume your original position. This flipping process can be done just once, but chances are that you'll need a few more hours … just to be sure it's dry! Hey, don't knock it until you've tried it.

7 Send out for supper, or let your special man cook (even if he's an awful cook, men look great in the kitchen – and food always tastes better when you don't have to cook it).

8 Bring the quilt indoors and let it spend its first night on a spare bed (this way you can be sure it's totally dry before you fold it and put it away).

Speaking of folding and putting away …over the years I've found that nearly everyone folds quilts the same way: in half and half again. After 33 years of quilt making I've found that rather noticeable folds have begun to appear on my older quilts.

Since I always folded each quilt the same way a rather nasty ridge has emerged on these fold lines which just will not go away. So, if you're putting your quilts away, please try to alternate your folding pattern and sometimes fold each quilt in threes. This method will put less strain on those central fold lines, and will add to the beauty and longevity of your lovely quilts.

Quilts can be washed in the washing machine, but only in cold water, and on a short, gentle cycle with a minimum of spinning. I stick to my bathtub method because I know I'll be able to see if any fabric begins to bleed and I can swiftly take action! (If your quilt *does* start to bleed – that is, to lose colour into the water – try adding a box of table salt or a bottle of clear white vinegar to the water; be careful **not** to put either of these products directly onto the quilt. Then add more cold water and pray …)

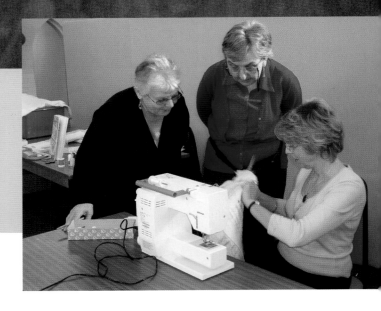

Tips You Cannot Possibly Do Without

Before I go on, I'd like to make one point very clear. If something makes sense, then give it a go! If it doesn't and you are happy with your current method or product, then by all means stick with it as that's the right way for you. So here we go. I'm not attempting to teach a duck to swim ... I just want him to know that there is a world out there beyond the pond!

Imperial or metric?

After endless days of hair-pulling and sleepless nights, I've decided *not* to try and translate the measurements in this book into metric. I feel that the imperial system (as cumbersome and awkward as it can be) has always been the 'language' of quiltmaking. And unfortunately, metric and imperial don't translate into neat equivalents. If only 4cm = 1in ... but it doesn't.

Against the grain ... or not?

First, let's examine the grain issue. Have you ever really thought about the way the grain of your fabric affects the final outcome of your quilt? Possibly not.

Our woven cotton patchwork fabrics are made by interlacing two sets of yarns at right angles to each other. There are generally 68 threads per square inch in each direction. Compare this to the densely-woven 180 count cotton percale used for fine sheets – this is why I don't recommend them as backings for quilts that are destined for hand quilting.

The selvedge edge runs along the **lengthwise** grain of the fabric on both sides. It's here that you often see little squares of colour, or the name of the fabric or the designer.

The selvedge is usually about ½in wide, and it's there so that the fabric can be stretched and printed without affecting the usable area of the fabric. Always remove this selvedge from your fabric so that it can never become a part of your quilt

This lengthwise grain is the most stable. It has very little stretch – and we can use this to our advantage.

Crosswise grain, which runs perpendicular to the selvedge, has a bit more stretch. And, of course, the most stretch comes from the bias, which is the exact 45° angle to each set of threads.

Take a piece of fabric out from your stash and try pulling it in these three directions. Quite a difference, isn't there!? Maybe now you can see why the direction of the grain can make such a difference in your work.

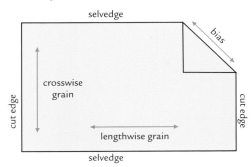

When cutting your pieces, position your templates so that the outside edges of blocks are always on grain (**a**). And, whenever possible, have a bias edge supported by a straight grain edge (**b**).

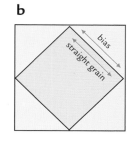

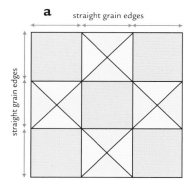

To cut or to tear?

Will you cut or tear your fabric? That is the loaded question …

Rotary cutting has probably done more to increase the speed and accuracy of quilts than any other one tool, but it does have its limitations. The one biggest draw back is that it really cannot cut accurately on the grain.

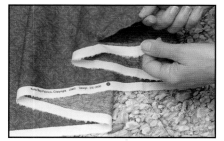

How many times have you bought just the amount you needed and then found you couldn't cut all your pieces from what you bought? Rotary cutting is the culprit. I know that some people cringe at the thought of tearing fabric, but once you understand how it can help you, you may then decide to do it as well.

Cotton fabric will always tear perfectly straight. Simply make a small cut to begin, then take a deep breath and rip away! To remove your selvedges do the same. You may want to keep the selvedges and one day crochet a rag rug from them. (Really! Get a big hook and keep going until you're bored.)

After ripping, some ladies feel that the ragged or 'distressed' edge they've torn is a problem. If so, then simply rip your strips a tiny bit wider than you actually need and tidy the edges up by cutting the frazzled bits off with a rotary cutter. You'll have a tidy strip, and it will be on grain.

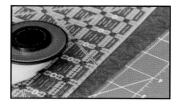

Quilt borders especially benefit from this. I always tear my border, from the **_lengthwise_** grain of my fabric. Yes, I do have to buy a bit more fabric, but I won't have to piece my border and ruin the frame of my quilt with seams. Even a very large quilt, for example 108in, only needs 3½ yards of fabric. You can get four 10in border strips out of that, and if your border is narrower you might also get the binding from that amount. The end result is a quilt bordered by fabric that is on grain, and so will drape and hang beautifully. It's also easier to hand quilt fabric that is on grain – an added bonus.

I also rip large squares for appliqué blocks. I tear them at least 2in larger than the size I need; that way, after stitching (which tends to pull the background in), I can press my block and then trim it down to the exact size I want with my rotary cutter.

Sashing strips also benefit from tearing. If they're on grain they will support the blocks even if the blocks themselves are not perfectly on grain. It's little things like this that make the difference between a quilt that looks a bit 'homemade,' and one that looks 'home crafted.'

Back to backings

A wee word about your backside … er … your backings! The front is finally finished, and now it's time to make the quilt sandwich. But what are you going to put on the back? Much of the answer to that question will depend upon the way you intend to quilt. If you're machine quilting you can choose pretty much any fabric, as the machine will be able to penetrate it. If you're new to machine quilting, I suggest that you use a busy print rather than a plain colour, as it's far more forgiving and will show fewer errors than plain (solid) fabric!

You can use 100% cotton sheets that match your bedding, or even incorporate spare blocks from the front design into the backing piece.

If you intend to do any hand quilting I would suggest that you stay with the same type of printed cotton fabric that you used on the front. Today you can buy a variety of fabrics that are 90in or 108in wide, so you don't have to piece the back. If you can't locate these extra-wide fabrics then you'll have to piece the backing, as our quilting fabrics only come 40 usable inches wide.

Please resist the temptation just to sew two lengths of fabric side by side to create a backing piece. Take a few extra moments, as doing it right will certainly pay off in the end.

Let's assume you have a quilt 70 x 90in. You will need 6yd of backing fabric.

1 Pre-wash the fabric, tear off the selvedges, lightly press, and then put a safety pin into the top of your fabric (**a**).

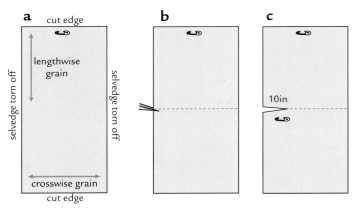

2 Measure down 3yd/108in, clip (**b**), and then tear from selvedge edge to selvedge edge. As you get about 10in into the tear, put in another safety pin at the top of the piece you are tearing (**c**). Continue tearing, and place another safety pin about 30in into the tear; finish tearing. You now have two 40 x 108in pieces (**d**). One has one pin at the top (this is your centre piece) and another has two safety pins at the top (this section will be divided to become your side pieces).

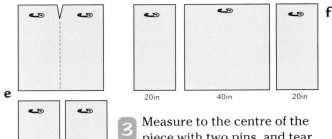

3 Measure to the centre of the piece with two pins, and tear it in half, down its length, along the **lengthwise** grain (**e**). You now have three strips. Lay them out in this order: 20in strip + 40in + 20in, making sure that each section has the pin at the top (**f**).

4 Place these three pieces right sides together with their pins at the top, and sew with a ½in seam allowance. I reduce my stitch length for this seam as I feel it deters the thread from showing through and keeps the wadding from creeping out!

The reason I make my backings this way is that fabric has a nap to it. It may not be as noticeable as it is in velvet or corduroy, but depending on the printing and dyeing process and the greige goods (base fabrics) used it may be quite noticeable if you flip one of the pieces over.

Sometimes it's only noticeable over the years as the quilt is washed, used, and is beginning to fade. So if you make sure that you piece the strips all in the same direction you'll never have this problem. Also, sewing a centre seam eventually shows through onto the front of your quilt. Out of habit we tend to fold our quilts down the centre, and as the wadding flattens, this long seam can begin to show through on the front of the quilt. To avoid this it's also worth trying to get into the habit of folding your quilt into thirds once in a while.

5 Press each seam once while shut, and then press the seam **open** (**g**). Yes, this is one of the few times I press a seam open; I feel it distributes the bulk better.

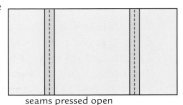

seams pressed open

6 Now give the back a final press; you may want to give the whole thing a spray with spray starch if you're going to machine quilt. And now you're ready to make your sandwich (hold the mayo!).

Phew! Those were all pretty heavy subjects. How about if I now offer you a few short but sweet tips that could save you time and improve the quality of your work?

The ever-elusive quarter-inch seam

Sew with a scant ¼in seam. It seems that a ¼in seam is something different to everyone! But in reality, pieced quilts are designed assuming that you'll produce a block made up of perfect, finished ¼in seams. Once you stop laughing, wipe your eyes and get up off the floor, I will proceed ...

Even with a quarter-inch foot you can get a seam that is very slightly wider or narrower than ¼in. Just stitching the width of your needle to the right or left can affect this. When you press your seam to the side a tiny amount of fabric, about 2-3 threads, is taken up in the pressing. The thickness of the thread also adds to the bulk. All of these things can affect the perfect ¼in.

Try cutting three strips of fabric 1½in wide. Sew them together as you currently sew a ¼in seam. When the seam's finished, press and measure the width. It should be 3½in. What does yours measure?

Prepare three more strips and try sewing with a scant ¼in. Or try using a ruler and mark a ¼in line on your fabric. What do these new strips measure?

Some quilters use a magnetic guide, masking tape or moleskin to create a guide that the fabric cannot go beyond. Find a method that works best for you and stick to it, as consistency is most important. Wouldn't it be wonderful actually to make a quilt that finishes up at exactly the size the pattern promises?

Keeping stitches on the straight and narrow

Want perfectly-formed stitches? Then replace your multi-stitch sole plate with a straight stitch plate. All sewing machines today are capable of doing a vast variety of multi-function stitches, so the sole plate that comes on your machine probably has an oval opening (**a**). This allows the needle to move to the left and right without it breaking on the sole plate.

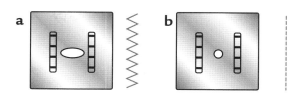

A straight stitch sole plate (**b**) has only a tiny hole, which allows the needle to go through but doesn't drag any fabric down with it. This dragging of fabric can cause skipped stitches or simply a bad stitch formation. When you are straight stitching while piecing, or when you're doing free-form quilting, a single hole sole plate helps produce a much better stitch.

Easy stitch removal

This section is all about how to make removing unwanted stitches as painless as possible. It seems such a frustrating waste of time, but it's far better to bite the bullet and fix the problem rather than trying to 'make it work.' It seldom does!

Careless removal of the stitches can cause more problems than you had originally. I have seen quilters cutting stitches away with scissors (arrgh!) or hacking through the seam with a seam ripper and mercilessly mangling the fabric (No! No! No!) Here is a simple, easy way to remove unwanted stitches without harming your fabric.

Go to the reverse side of the stitching (the side that was against the feed dogs) and, with a good-quality seam ripper, cut through every fourth stitch (**a**). When this is done, go to the front of the work and gently pull on the top thread (**b**). As if by magic, the top thread comes away in one piece and the bottom bobbin threads just fall away. You can now place tape on the loose threads (**c**) and they will disappear with hardly a trace. No distortion to the fabric, and no loose threads to clean up. Yippee!

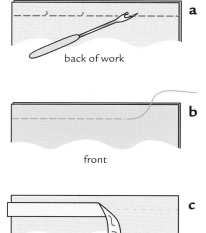

back of work

front

back

Sorry, no ironing!

Quilters 'press' … we do not 'iron' (nor do we do buttons!).

Ironing is for shirts, sheets and for things we wear to impress. It usually involves steam and a whole lot of sliding around.

Quilters press. We press seams after stitching them. We press blocks to square them and flatten them. We even press our tops to ready them for quilting. This pressing is done with a firm up-and-down motion and shouldn't involve any steam.

If you choose to starch your work, spray lightly and allow the starch to melt into the fabric. Quite often in their enthusiasm quilters spray and press within seconds of each other. Then they wonder why there seems to be dandruff on their fabric. What they've done is basically cooked the starch before it's had a chance to be absorbed by the fabric.

Yes, you definitely must press. When in doubt, press: but do so carefully. Perfect piecing can indeed be ruined by over-zealous pressing.

For the best results, press each seam twice. Double pressing gives a very crisp, flat seam. Once the seam is sewn, take it to the ironing board and press the pieces together with a hot, dry iron; this 'sets' the threads into the fabric and flattens the seam. I always press with the piece on top that will have the seam pressed towards it. For example: If I'm sewing peach and white pieces together I will place the white on the ironing board and the peach piece on top. After the first pressing I simply 'open the door', lay the iron onto the white piece, and as I'm sliding the iron I'm pressing the seam to the peach piece.

Pressing on a grid

You can press your pieces much more accurately if you have an ironing board cover that has a grid on it. You can line your strips up and press them straight; you can also sew half-square triangles together and press them into a perfect square.

If you can't find a gridded cover ready-made, you can buy a plain one and use your ruler and a **permanent** felt-tipped pen to make your own. June Tailor makes Cut & Press Mats with a grid printed on them; these are so much more useful than press mats with a twee print …

Making successful fabric choices

I think the thing most quilters are afraid of is choosing their fabrics for a quilt. Although this can be the most fun part, it does make some people's blood run cold! I have a simple philosophy: think of choosing the fabrics for your quilt as if you were casting a West-End musical. You will need a *star*, some *co-stars*, and the *bit players* or *chorus line*.

The star

Find one fabric you love. It should be a print with an interesting design or theme, and it should contain several colours. This fabric will set the tone of the quilt, and will most certainly be the one noticed first and most often. For example:

The co-stars

Now look at the star fabric and take note of the basic colours. Find other fabrics that are in these colours but which are not too flashy. Collect various prints and values of colour; look for fabrics that support and enhance the star without taking over the spotlight (heaven forbid!) For example:

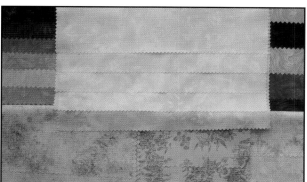

The chorus line

Without these guys you just don't have a show. They shouldn't attract much attention, though; if they do, you just have a stage full of egocentrics all fighting for centre stage. These are your neutrals, your background fabrics. The more the merrier; in *Listen To The Leaves Singing* I used heaps of bit players. Why choose one tone-on-tone beige when you can have dozens!?

Values

Also remember you need ***dark darks*** and ***light lights*** to make all those mediums look good! Just because you have ten different colours doesn't necessarily mean that you have ten different values. If you have trouble seeing value try using a 'value finder'. This is a piece of red plastic which you look through; as you look,  the plastic filter has the effect of removing the colours from your fabrics and just leaving you with the values. This allows you to see just how light or dark each fabric is. Lack of contrast is often why one quilt says ZING! (see above) while another just seems to be whimpering in the corner.

How much do I buy?

Let's be honest: as often as not we impulse-buy fabric before we ever know what we'll do with it! It is just so darn beautiful, or unique, or such a great deal that it really demands to be brought home. The question 'Do I need it?' (do birds need to fly?) never enters our heads. What we *do* need advice on is just how much to buy when the time comes.

I have a simple formula. I buy:

- ½yd if it is truly unique, very expensive, or just plain weird (but I love it!)

- 1yd if it's a potential star fabric

- 2yd if it's a neutral background (chorus line) fabric for blocks or appliqué

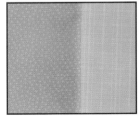

- 3yd if it would be a great border, or sashing and binding (co-star)

- 6yd if it's at a reduced price and has potential as a backing (usually a subtle print)

If your fabric stash is building, you may want to take a moment and do an honest inventory.

- Do you have some of every colour? (I do find it impossible to buy p-i-n-k. Just don't like it!)

- Do you have light, medium and dark values in all these colours?

- Do you have too many 'stars' and no 'chorus line'?

- Do you have some stripes and plaids?

Make a list of what you really need and put it in your purse. That way, the next time you stumble into a shop you'll have a basic idea of what you should be allowing to follow you home!

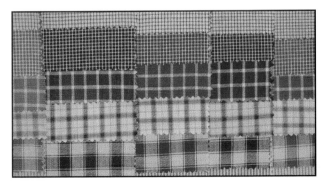

Aunt Helen's easy bias stems

Later on in the pattern section you'll get to meet my Aunt Helen. She's gone now, but her life was one of simplicity and no fuss. Although the Clover company now makes nifty bias-strip makers in several widths, Aunt Helen had a way to make them with nothing more than her ironing board and two pins. Here is her method:

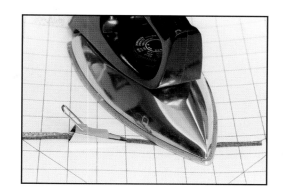

1 Cut bias strips of your fabric **three times the finished width** of the bias stems you need. (So, for a ½in bias stem, cut bias strips 1½in wide.)

2 Lightly spray the strips with spray starch (lightly – not dripping wet!) Place one strip on your ironing board with the wrong side facing up. Gently fold the first 8in or so into thirds and press only this bit dry (**a**).

3 Insert a long, yellow-headed pin through the ironing board cover, bring the pin over the pre-folded strip and reinsert it into the ironing board cover immediately after it clears the folded strip (**b**).

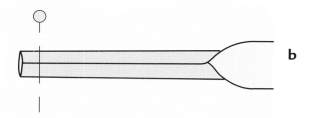

4 Place a second pin about 4-5in to the right of the first (**c**). **These pins must not be inserted into the strips**.

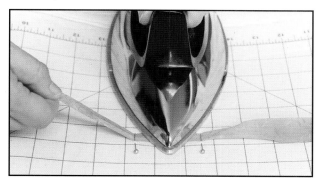

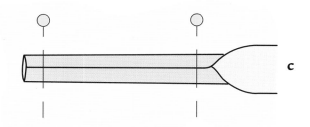

Place your iron over the strip between the pins and gently pull on the beginning part of the strip. As the unfolded fabric contacts the pin it will automatically fold over and you will iron it closed as the iron passes over it (**d**).

5 Keep an eye on the strip as it's pulled, and work slowly. Every once in a while pick up the iron and let your board cool so that you don't scorch your cover.

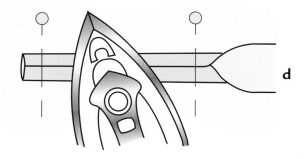

The beauty of this technique is that you can make *any* size bias, *any* time you want, and there's *nothing* extra to buy!

A Recap Of The IMA Technique

In this section, I'm offering a brief recap of the technique for those of you who have never done IMA, or for those who don't have the first book. For more detailed instructions, please refer to IMA Book One.

Setting up your machine for Invisible Machine Appliqué

You will need:

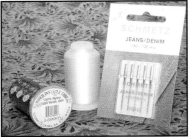

- an all-cotton, neutral-coloured thread in 50/3, 50/2 or 40/2 weight

- Denim/Jeans or Sharps needles, one 80/12 and one 70/10

- YLI Invisible Thread

- a roughly 10in square scrap of plain, dark fabric for your practice stitches

1 Fill your bobbin with the same cotton thread you're using on the top.

2 Insert the 80/12 needle into the machine.

3 Thread the machine with the cotton thread (we'll go invisible after you create your personal, perfect stitch)

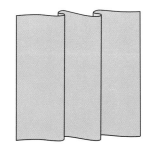

4 Press two pleats into your dark fabric as shown.

5 Set your machine for the blind hem stitch. It looks like this: ⅄⅄⅄⅄⅄⅄

If you don't have this stitch, see the stitch update on pages 7-8.

Do not use the blind hemming foot. We're not actually hemming. You could use your normal sewing foot, but I strongly suggest that you invest in an open-toe foot (it may be called an open-toe embroidery foot). You can see in the photographs what it looks like; the centre bar has been removed to give you a clear view of what you are sewing.

You cannot use your ¼in foot, nor can you use your darning foot. A clear appliqué foot is a possibility, but it still has that bar in the way, even if it's clear!

Beginning to stitch

1 Position your fabric under the machine foot so that the fold is to the left of your needle. (This is assuming that your machine 'bites' – makes the little V-shaped stitches – to the left. Most of them do. If your machine 'bites' to the right you'll have to put your fold on that side.)

We're using the folded edge as if it were an appliqué motif. Whenever you try a new stitch, it's best to do it under exactly the same conditions, and with the same materials, as you'll be working with when you're actually sewing.

2 Stitch so that the straight lines of the stitch are on the background (single layer) of the fabric right next to the fold. Only the bite goes over onto the fold, as shown here.

The stitch will be very large, as the machine thinks you really are going to be hemming. But we know differently! Now we'll adjust the stitch width and length to produce your own individual IMA stitch.

3 First reduce your **width** until it looks roughly like this:

You want the bite to just nibble on the fold. This little V-shaped bite holds your appliqué onto the background fabric, so be sure it catches every time.

4 Stop sewing and reduce your stitch **length**. Note how the bites are getting closer together. Reduce the length until it looks roughly like this:

(If you're having trouble adjusting to a suitable length, see the section on sewing machines, page 7.)

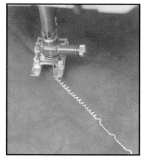

I can't give you an exact size for these stitches as every machine is different, and everyone sees the stitches differently. Most people have their width and length somewhere around the 1-1.25 or 1.5 range.

When you find the settings you like, write them down. You don't want to have to go through this process every time!

Going invisible ...

1 Replace the cotton thread on top of the machine with a clear monofilament thread (leave the cotton in the bobbin).

2 Replace your needle with the size 70/10.

3 Stitch down the second fold for a few inches.

4 Remove the fabric from your machine and let's have a critique of the stitching.

- Has the thread sewn successfully on your machine?

- Do you see any of the bobbin thread on the top of your work?

- If so, is it just a wee bit which I fondly call 'snow flurries,' or do you have a blizzard!?

Suggestions for getting rid of snow

- Reduce your upper tension one number at a time until the snow 'melts.'

- If you have a Bernina you can thread your bobbin thread through the 'finger' on the bobbin case. This little hole is unique to Berninas; using it slightly tightens the bobbin tension without you having to touch the screw. Excellent for buttonholes and satin stitch appliqué.

- On machines other than Berninas, try tightening your bobbin screw (see page 13).

- You could also replace your neutral thread with a medium grey thread to blend better with the dark background fabric.

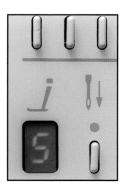

Smart tip! Set your machine to stop in the **needle down** position if you have this facility on your machine; it will help when you're appliquéing curves.

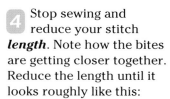

Preparing your fabric for appliqué

Your machine can now do a lovely appliqué stitch, but what it cannot do is turn the edges under on your appliqué motif as it stitches. So you'll have to prepare each piece before you stitch it down. There are several ways to do this. I find different

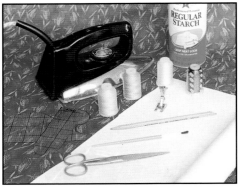

appliqués require different techniques; you may use them all or choose your favourite. I suggest that you make one sample using each method and see what you think.

You will need:

- one 10in square of background fabric
- two 5in squares of appliqué fabric (for the hearts)
- two 5in squares of freezer paper (for the hearts)
- one 2½ x 5in piece of freezer paper (for the Dresden Plate)
- one 3 x 7in strip of iron-on Vilene, medium weight (for the Dresden Plate)
- three 3½ x 5in pieces of three different fabrics
- your sewing machine
- spray starch and a small, cheap paintbrush
- pencil
- scissors, pins, iron (dry is better than steam)
- clear invisible and neutral cotton threads

Method 1: freezer paper and spray starch

My favourite, and probably the one you'll use most often.

1. Trace the heart shape (right) onto freezer paper and cut it out. Place your appliqué fabric on the ironing board, wrong side up.

2. Set the iron on cotton. Place the freezer paper heart on the fabric with the paper side up (the shiny side is in contact with the fabric), and press the heart onto the fabric (**a**).

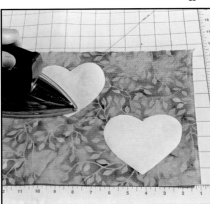

a

3. Spray some spray starch into the cap or a small dish. (Don't use fabric finish or anything that claims to make wrinkles disappear. These products contain silicone and will not hold a crisp edge. Use pure starch.)

b

With your paintbrush paint a quarter inch of starch all around the freezer paper shape.

4. Cut out the fabric a scant ¼in away from the heart (**b**).

Heart template
for Methods 1 and 2

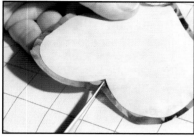

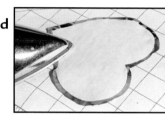
d

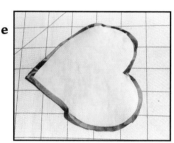
e

c

With either of the above methods, if you make a mistake, simply press the seam allowance flat and begin again. Take your time. You should be able to get a beautiful smooth edge. If yours is lumpy, try cutting a slightly smaller seam allowance.

Method 3: Lining with iron-on interfacing

This technique is best when you need to appliqué a pieced appliqué. That is: when you've sewn several bits of fabric together and you want to appliqué the whole unit. For example:

- You've made some crazy patchwork and want to cut it out and appliqué it as a heart.

- You've made a New York Beauty or Crown of Thorns block (see page 94).

- You're making a Dresden Plate quilt.

- Anytime you have more than one fabric in a piece and you want to appliqué it as a unit.

To show you how this technique works, try this sample piece with a section of a Dresden Plate design.

5 You'll need to make three small clips in the dip of the heart (**c**). Always clip in dips, never on an outside curve.

6 Begin pressing on the straight edge of the heart (**d**), and press the wet seams up and over onto the freezer paper. Be sure to let the starch dry completely. Fold the tip over as shown (**e**).

Method 2: Freezer paper shiny side up

1 Draw another heart on the freezer paper and cut it out.

2 Place your appliqué fabric on the ironing board wrong side up.

3 Put the freezer paper heart on the appliqué fabric with the paper side against the wrong side of the fabric. Pin in place (**a**).

a

4 Carefully cut the out the fabric ¼in from the freezer paper. Clip your inside curves as before.

5 Take the unit to the ironing board and press the seam allowance up and over onto the shiny side of the freezer paper (**b**). The freezer paper will not harm your iron. I promise!

b
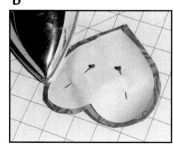

1 Trace the Dresden plate shape below onto freezer paper and cut it out.

2 Place three different fabrics in a pile and iron the Dresden Plate wedge onto the top piece (**a**). Cut out the fabrics around the template. (Don't add a seam allowance – it's already built into the template.)

a

Dresden Plate template
for Method 3

3 Sew the three pieces together with a ¼in seam allowance and press the seams to the right as shown (**b**).

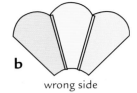
b
wrong side

4 Place the pieced unit right side down onto the interfacing (**c**), laying it on the side *without* the glue. **This is most important!** If you put your fabric onto the glue side you'll ruin your iron …

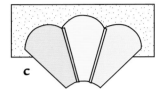
c

5 Reduce your stitch length to the shortest straight stitch your machine will comfortably sew. Stitch ¼in from the top edge of your pieced units with this tiny stitch (**d**); this will lock the threads of the fabrics so tightly together that they will never fray.

d
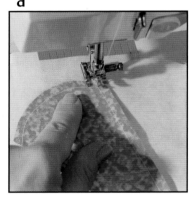

6 Now comes the scary part. Carefully cut the fabric and interfacing away to what I call 'SCARY CLOSE.' This is not an actual measurement, but a guide. You will cut to within a hair's breadth of your stitching (**e**); this way there will be no unsightly ridge made by the seam allowance.

But be warned! As one student moaned after cutting through her stitching, 'The distance between "scary" and "OOPS" is very small!' Think scary, not terrifying!

e

7 Turn the piece right side out. DO NOT cut away the remaining interfacing. Place the fabric side of the unit onto the ironing board and gently tug on the interfacing until you can see a halo of fabric along the top of the interfacing.

f
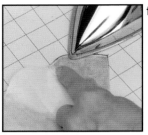

g

8 With the side of a hot, dry iron press the interfacing to the reverse side of the piecing, just along the edges of the shape (**f**). Now trim away the excess interfacing (**g**) and your piece is ready to appliqué (**h**).

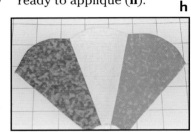
h

Stitching Invisible Machine Appliqué

1 Place one of your prepared pieces on your background fabric. Pin in place; I suggest using fine silk pins as they distort the fabric less than thicker pins.

2 Begin stitching on a straight section of your appliqué. With hearts, never begin in the dip or at the point as you'll then finish stitching there, and that creates a weak spot. The long side of the heart is the best place to start (**a**).

* begin
a

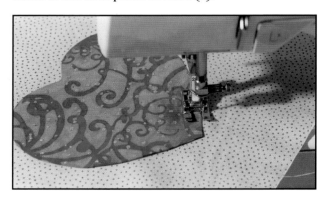

3 Make sure that the straight stitches are right next to the appliqué but not on it; only the bites will touch the appliqué (right).

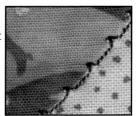

4 Using an open-toe foot will help you to see where you are stitching and help you avoid stitching on the appliqué itself. (If you do stitch up onto the appliqué motif a bit, 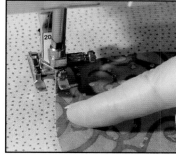 don't worry. No-one's perfect, and the thread is so invisible that it will probably never be noticed! Promise yourself to do better next time …)

5 There's no special trick to starting and stopping. Just begin stitching, and when you get to the end, stitch over your first stitches for about 1in and then cut the threads flush with the fabric. If you wish you may back-stitch, but only do this after a run of straight stitches and not at a bite.

6 Now carefully cut away the background fabric from behind your appliqué and remove the freezer paper. I find that it comes away more easily if you pull a small amount away from the stitching and then run your finger between the fabric and the freezer paper to break the bond. Then the freezer paper can be 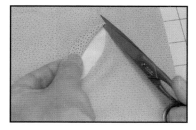 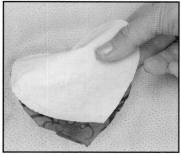 removed from the stitching as easily as a cheque comes out of a cheque book. And we all know how easy that is!

Now sit back and admire
your beautiful work.
It was fun (I hope!) …
it looks great … .
and you did it all yourself!

PROJECTS

Now, how about having a look at some quilts you can make using IMA? In each section I've suggested a way to use IMA, then given you instructions for a project you can use to try out your new skill.

Enjoy!

Some basic facts hold true throughout this section:

- For the yardages I've given, I'm assuming that all fabrics have 40 usable inches from selvedge to selvedge.

- The appliqué templates do not have seam allowances included, unless specified (for example the Drunkard's Path template)

- Please sew all seams with a scant ¼in seam allowance.

- Choose a wadding to suit the end use of your quilt. I use Mountain Mist Quilt-Light for my hand-quilted quilts, and a variety of waddings for my machine-quilted quilts. (See the section on waddings/battings on pages 14-16 for more details.)

- Please feel free to change or adapt each pattern to make it your own!

When was the last time you did something for the very first time?

Come on! Challenge yourself and try something new!

We both know you can do it …

Inset Seams

Windows To Provence *2003*

Just How Many Frogs Do
I Have To Kiss?! *2004*

Number one new use for IMA: think about using it to solve those awkward piecing problems!

In Book One I suggested that you IMAed your appliquéd blocks onto the background fabric to avoid difficult mitring situations. Why not take the idea further and use IMA to help you avoid having to inset pieces?

Two patterns immediately come to mind: Star of Bethlehem (**a**), and Attic Windows (**b**). For each method, you have to contend with inset seams – inserting a patch into a 90° angle (**c**).

Star of Bethlehem

If you follow the traditional way of piecing Star of Bethlehem, you finish piecing your star, and then have to make quarter-square triangles and squares to finish it off (**d**).

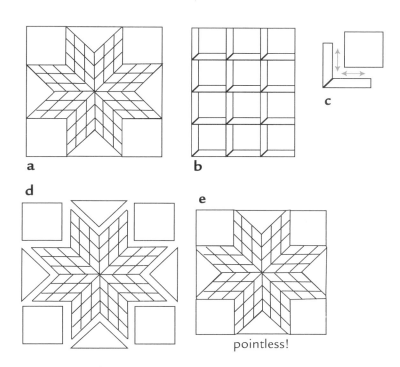

Denver Nights *1994*

This is not fun. Trust me. I would much rather prepare my quarter-square triangles and squares with the freezer paper and spray starch method (see page 36), and then IMA them onto the pieced star! It's faster and easier, and the star generally lays much flatter. (I wouldn't suggest IMAing the star onto a fabric background, as there are so many seams it would frustrate me no end, but if you can make it work, great!)

Always cut your quarter-square triangles and squares much larger than you think you will need. This way you can always trim them down if you don't want them to 'float,' but if you make them to size and they are even a smidge too small, you will then cut off your points (e) and end up with a very dull-looking star indeed!

Attic Windows

Attic Windows need inset seams to piece the window into the block, but IMA makes it so much easier. Attic Windows are endlessly versatile, and fun as well. You can use them for quilts and for large or small wall-hangings; you can make them in contemporary or traditional styles, and they make good use of those novelty prints we often buy but can never find a use for (**a**)!

As this design is so much easier to make using IMA, you can quickly fill your windows with pre-printed fabrics, photo transfers, pieced blocks, embroidery, counted cross stitch or appliqué. You'll hardly get one finished before you find yourself planning another one! You can make your windows very tiny and frame them, or make them large and sleep under them. The only trick to remember is that you must always have three colour values: light, medium and dark.

These three different colour values can be arranged in various different ways in your basic Attic Windows block, as shown on the right.

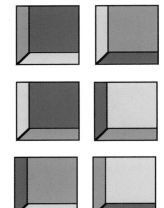

The examples below show how the idea works with fabric. In **b** and **c** the window effect is lost, because there isn't enough contrast among the three fabric patches. Examples **d**, **e** and **f** all work well, even though the colour values are in different parts of the design. The final sample (**g**) shows that even with three very different prints, the sense of depth is lost when the fabrics don't have sufficiently different colour values.

a

An attic window design by Dr Cathy Corbishley

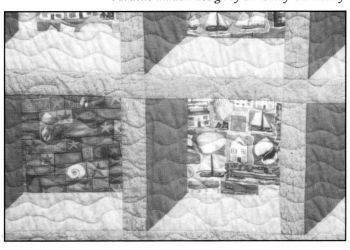

b   **c**

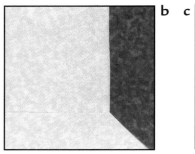

d   **e**

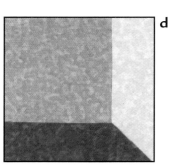
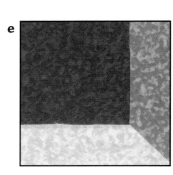

f   **g**

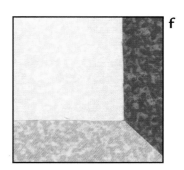

You're trying to create the illusion that you're inside a room, looking out through a window to a scene of your own making. And what will you put in your window? How about collecting fabrics featuring your favourite animal or sport or hobby, and filling your windows with them? You could make a fabric album of holiday shots or treasured baby or wedding photos. Or use pre-printed fabrics of a landscape scene, as I did with *Windows to Provence*, and add a view to a windowless room. The possibilities are endless!

One horizontal and one vertical window-sill are sewn onto two sides of each 'window.' A general rule to follow is to keep the width of your sills no more than one third of the window's width. Why not get out some graph paper and a pencil, and try a few different sizes to see what happens?

Our wisteria window at Rosenannon, Kent

Your windows can be square (**h**) or rectangular (**i**), depending on what suits your fabric best.

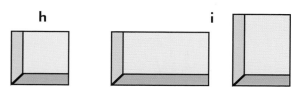

You can also add a window-frame for added depth. If you fancy doing this, it's usually best to keep the frame fabric plain and make sure that it's a good contrast to the sills; the illustrations show how different the same design looks without (**j**) and with (**k**) extra window-frames.

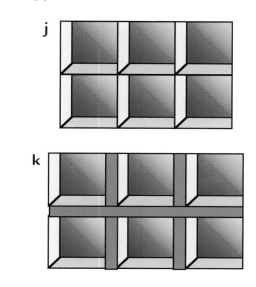

You could also let some of the elements of your design come out onto the window-sill (like the frog below); use bonding web, or IMA, or hand appliqué to secure the shape in place.

Windows To Provence

Do you or a friend work in a windowless cubicle?
Have you recently seen fabric featuring a lovely landscape,
but couldn't imagine what to do with it?
This wall-hanging may be a way to bring a little sunshine into your life!

Quilt dimensions: 43 x 38in

You will need:

For the windows

❖ ½yd pretty countryside print fabric (or more if you want to choose specific areas to cut out)

For the window-sills

❖ ¼yd light fabric
❖ ¼yd medium fabric

For the window-frame

❖ ¼yd dark fabric

For the border

❖ 1½yd

For finishing

❖ 1¼yd for the backing (used horizontally)
❖ ½yd for the binding

Other requirements

❖ 1¼yd wadding/batting (a needle-punched cotton wadding would hang well)
❖ 1yd freezer paper (you could make do with less if you re-use the paper shapes)
❖ stapler
❖ pencil, ruler
❖ spray starch and brush
❖ **threads:** 100% cotton for piecing, YLI Wonder Invisible for IMA, YLI Machine Quilting for free-form machine quilting (I also did some hand quilting on the landscapes with YLI Hand Quilting)

Preparation

From the window fabric, cut nine 8½ x 6½in window shapes. (Remember that only the centre 8 x 6in will show, so choose your views carefully.)

You'll need about 240in of 1in strips for the window-frame; cut these selvedge to selvedge as needed.

I suggest that you tear the fabric for the borders – see page 27; you'll need two 6½ x 46in strips for the vertical border, and two 6½ x 41in for the horizontal border. My border had directional lavender 'growing' on it, so I used a 1⅛yd piece and IMAed the windows unit onto it.

Making the quilt top

1 Fold the freezer paper in half (waxy sides together) and trace the sill template (**A**) onto the paper nine times. Put a staple into the centre of each shape (**a**), so that you're stapling the two layers together, and cut out the shapes; you now have nine sets/pairs of sills (**b**). (Folding and stapling the paper like this ensures that you end up with pairs of mirror-image templates.)

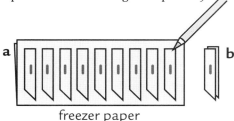

freezer paper

2 On each set of sills, label the side you drew on: '2 – side.' Label the side with the back of the staple '1 – bottom.' Remove the staples but keep the pairs together (**c**).

3 Lay the medium fabric right side down on your ironing board and press the nine '2 – side' freezer paper templates, waxy side down, onto the reverse of the fabric, leaving at least ¼in seam allowance around each template (**d**). Repeat the process with the light fabric with the '1 – bottom' templates (**e**). Cut out all 18 shapes, leaving ¼in seam allowance all around each paper template (**f**).

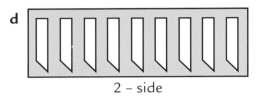

d

2 – side

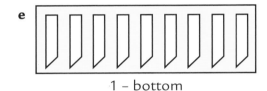

e

1 – bottom

1 – bottom   f   2 – side

4 Place one light and one medium sill right sides together. Use a positioning pin (stuck straight into the fabric, not flat in the usual way) at each end of the template as shown (**g**). Pin the main part of the seam in the usual way.

g   1 – bottom

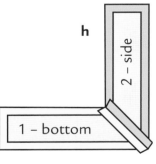

h   2 – side   1 – bottom

5 Stitch the seam from one end of the freezer paper to the other; press the seam open (**h**). You now have a right-angled sill.

6 Paint the inside seam allowances with spray starch and press them to the freezer paper (**i**). (For more details of how to do this, see Method 1 on page 36.)

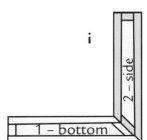

i   2 – side   1 – bottom

7 Spray-starch the window patch to add body to the fabric, and lay it right side up. Position the sill unit right side up onto the patch, ¼in in from the window edge, and IMA in place (**j**). Press the block well and square it up if necessary; remove the freezer paper shapes. Repeat the process with all the other pairs of sills and window patches to create nine blocks.

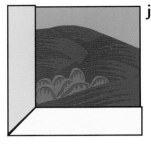

j

8 Sew the 1in frame strips between sets of three blocks (**k**), then between the rows and at the top and bottom of the design (**l**); make sure that all your windows are the same way up! Finally, add frame strips to each side of the design (**m**), then add the borders (**n**). In my quilt the border fabric was strongly directional (the lavender sprigs grew upwards in bundles), so I left it in one piece and 'appliquéd my appliqué' (see Book One page 36).

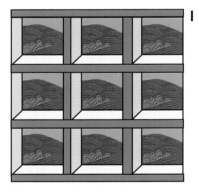

k

l   m

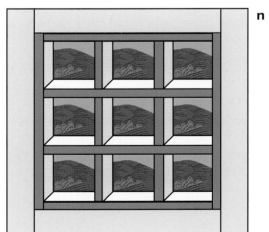

n

Finishing

1 Layer the quilt top with the wadding and backing and quilt as you wish by hand or machine. I hand-quilted my window scenes to give more definition to the topography (below).

2 Cut five 3½in strips for the bindings and sew on following the instructions on page 20 to finish the quilt.

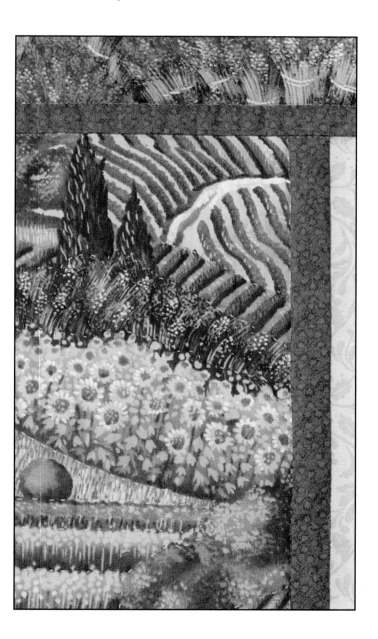

Template A
Attic Window sill
cut 9 mirror-image
pairs of sills
from freezer paper

Not-Quite-Invisible Machine Appliqué

Another name for this technique is Not-So-Very-IMA! To do it I use the buttonhole stitch (as suggested on page 8), but not the invisible thread. For the butterflies in the project I replaced the invisible thread with a YLI thread called Jeans Stitch, to appliqué and enhance the edges of the butterflies. This thread is thicker, and so provides a lovely hand-done looking stitch. Use a 90/14 topstitch needle for best results, and a 60/2 cotton in the bobbin. I also *increased* the stitch size.

You could also use Kaleidoscope or a metallic to give your butterflies a really flashy finish (below), or a rayon thread for slightly shiny ones!

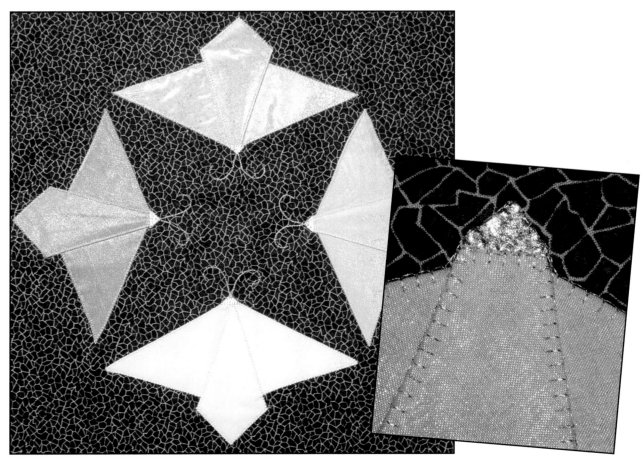

Nana's Butterflies

From 1942-45 my mother Lorraine Sobczak (nee Lewandowski) worked at John E Fast in Chicago, Illinois. They made electric condensers for the war effort. The girls who worked there were young and all lived on a limited budget so, on their birthdays, they agreed only to buy each other pretty handkerchiefs.

Over the years Mom's collection grew. I felt it was such a shame to see her collection languishing unused in her drawer, so one day a few years ago I began imagining these lovely squares folded into butterflies. I saw them flying free from the drawer into a beautiful summer sky. This quilt is the result.

I bet you have a collection you may have begun or inherited. Why not let these memories emerge from their cocoon and provide you with a unique quilt or wall-hanging? If you're short of handkerchiefs you could use hemmed squares of some of your beautiful fabrics.

Quilt dimensions: 74in square

You will need:

For the blocks and final border

❖ 3½yd background (sky) fabric (add an extra yard if you'd like a matching binding)

For the sashing

❖ 1½yd. I used a printed border; if you choose to do the same you will need about 425 running inches of the 3½in print

For the butterflies

❖ nine cotton handkerchiefs 12in square or smaller

❖ lightweight iron-on interfacing (optional)

❖ scraps of coloured felt for the butterflies' heads

❖ **thread:** Jeans Stitch or your own choice for the appliqué

For the backing

❖ 4½yd

Other requirements

❖ 1yd fabric for making the binding if you're not using the sky fabric

❖ 74in square wadding

❖ **threads:** 100% cotton for piecing, your own preferred threads for quilting by hand or machine

Preparation

From the background fabric, cut:

– nine 14¼in squares

– four 10 x 74in strips for the final border

From the sashing fabric cut:

– four 3½ x 55in strips

– four 3½ x 31½in strips

– four 3½ x 14¼in strips

Press each background block in half diagonally twice, and press the fold line lightly; unfold.

Creating the butterfly blocks

1 Hand wash and spray-starch all the handkerchiefs (or 'butterfly' fabric squares); make sure that they press square. If the hankies are very old, frail or too transparent you may wish to line them with a lightweight iron-on interfacing (below); I did this with all of mine and I found that it also helped to keep the shapes flat when I was appliquéing them.

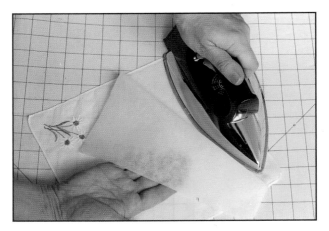

2 Fold each handkerchief or butterfly square in half diagonally. If the handkerchief has a pretty embroidered hem you might want to offset the fold a bit, so that the edges overlap slightly (**a**).

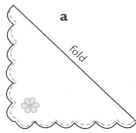

3 Pin the folded handkerchief to your ironing board with one pin in the very centre of the fold (**b**). Depending on the design on the handkerchief, find a good place about 2-3½in up from the corner and tuck the 'wing' in about 1in (**c**). This pleat will form the body and tail of the butterfly. Repeat on the other side (**d**). Sometimes this requires a bit of fiddling, and all your butterflies may be slightly different – just as they are in nature!

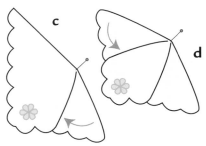

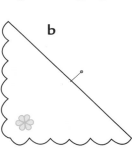

4 Once you're satisfied with the look of your butterfly, spray-starch it and pin it along the folds. Move the butterfly to a background block and line it up using the fold lines as a guide (**e**). Later you'll add an embroidered head and antennae, so allow for that when you place the butterfly in the block!

5 You could IMA your butterfly invisibly, but I liked the old-fashioned look of the buttonhole stitch. YLI Jeans Stitch thread and a 90/14 topstitch needle should give you a lovely hand-done look with either the blind hem or buttonhole stitch – try them out on a scrap fabric first, as you may want to enlarge the stitch width. Match or contrast the thread to the design on the handkerchief.

6 Cut a tiny felt triangle for the butterfly's head. I put a dab of fabric glue on the head to hold it in place while I did the appliqué. First stitch the base of the head triangle, then go to the asterisk and sew around to the dot (**f**). Continue stitching around the body and end at the dot. Make up the other butterfly blocks in the same way.

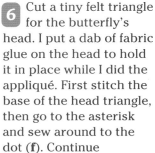

7 When all the blocks are appliquéd, hand-embroider the antennae with the Jeans Stitch thread (**g**). I used a wrapped chain stitch; stitch a normal chain stitch then go back down the chain weaving in and out of the chains to create a slightly stronger look (**h**).

Piecing a woven sashing

Lay your blocks out in a pleasing fashion and add your sashing strips in the order shown (**i-m**). This will create a cleaver woven appearance on the central panel (**n**).

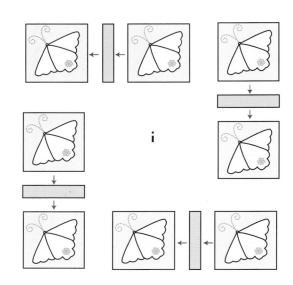

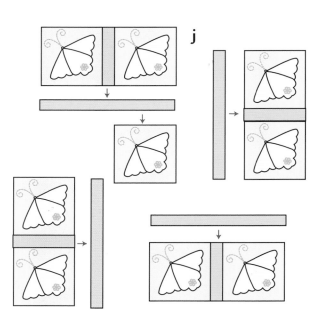

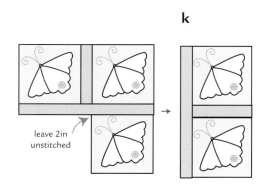

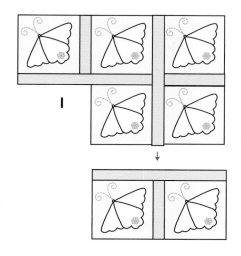

l

At stage **j**, attach the central butterfly square to the bottom edge of the sashing strip, beginning 2in in from the left-hand edge of the centre square. This will give you the leeway to add the final unit to the left-hand side of the square in step **m**.

Quilting and finishing

Stitch the long sashing strips to your border strips and sew these onto the quilt top, mitring the corners (**o**). (Easy mitring is covered in more detail in Book One.) Piece your backing according to the instructions on page 28, then layer your quilt 'sandwich' and quilt as desired. Bind the edges to complete your quilt.

m

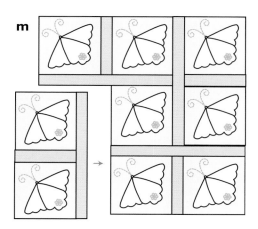

o

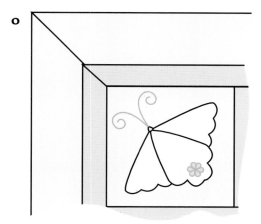

These butterflies will dry your tears and make all your sorrows fly away!

n

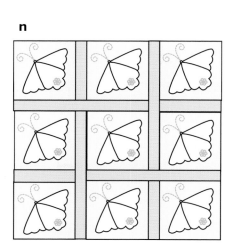

Reverse Appliqué and Peep-Holes

I had used reverse appliqué in the past when I was making Mariners Compass blocks, but it only recently occurred to me that the same idea could be used anytime when circles needed to be appliquéd to a background. It's just so much easier to press a seam back out on itself (**a**) rather than trying to press it smoothly in on itself around the circle (**b**). It's the same principle as putting a mat of mounting board over a photo or painting.

After working with the idea for a while I began calling the reverse circles peep-holes. As with Attic Windows, there are endless possibilities of what you can put inside your peep-holes; you could use photos printed on fabric, cross stitch, appliqué or novelty fabric prints. In *Find My Friend* (opposite) I've put two each of similar animal fabrics into the holes, and invite the wee ones to find the pairs.

Ra! *2003*

There's so much you can do with this idea. In *Ra!* (below, left) I used various orange fabrics to create the impression of the Egyptian sun god; the quilt uses much larger peep-holes, and a variety of orange fabrics to represent the sun. You could also strip-piece units and place your peep-holes over them (**c**). Wouldn't people be impressed!

Even tiny peep-holes are fun and easy to work with. Most certainly easier than trying to press edges over a circle! And it doesn't only have to be circles. How about hearts or ovals? Any curved shape would work (**d**).

Find My Friend

Children love bright colours and animals. In this quilt your favourite wee person can spend hours learning their colours by name, and also finding the matching animals. Every peep-hole contains an animal who has a friend somewhere on the quilt. You could also try replacing the animals with photographs of family members transferred onto fabric. Then you could play 'Where is Grandpa?', 'Can you find Grandma?' and so on. The fun never ends!

Quilt dimensions: 40in square

You will need:

For the background
❖ 1¼yd blue fabric

For the border and binding
❖ 1¼yd

For the backing
❖ 1¼yd

For the peep-holes
❖ 1yd freezer paper
❖ 5½in squares of 16 different multi-coloured fabrics
❖ 5½in squares of 8 different animal prints, two squares of each.

It's worth spending some time finding the right kind of fabrics to show through the peep-holes. The circular opening is about 3½in in diameter. Try making a paper 5in *finished* block, cut out the hole, and use that to audition fabrics. Some prints are just too big to fit comfortably inside the circle; others are too small and can get lost.

Other requirements
❖ 40in square of wadding (a cotton or poly/cotton blend would be nice)
❖ stapler
❖ template plastic
❖ spray starch and brush
❖ threads: 100% cotton for piecing, YLI Wonder Invisible for IMA and some quilting, and YLI Machine Quilting for the machine quilting

Making the peep-holes

1 Trace template **A** onto template plastic and cut out. Cut sixteen 5½in squares of freezer paper; fold each square into quarters and use the peep-hole template to mark the area you'll cut out. Draw around the template (**a**), staple the layers together (**b**) and cut out (**c**). Remove the staple and unfold the square (**d**): voilà! One peep-hole.

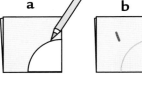

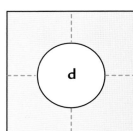

2 Iron one freezer paper peep-hole, waxy side down, onto the reverse side of each of the 16 squares of fabric (**e**). Cut the spare fabric away inside the circle to within ¼in of the freezer paper (**f**).

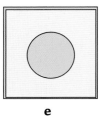
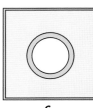

3 Paint the seam allowance with spray starch, then clip the seam allowance carefully to

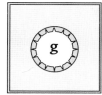 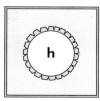

within a few threads of the freezer paper (**g**). Press this clipped seam up and over the freezer paper (**h**).

4 You now have a fabric peep-hole 'mat'; place this mat right side up on one square of animal fabric and 'shop around' for the perfect composition (**i**). Don't worry about the grain line … your animals will be securely appliquéd. What is most important is that they look good (see below)!

 Because the square blocks are going to be set 'on point,' you might find that some motifs look best when they're slightly angled inside the circle.

5 When you're happy with the positioning, IMA the circular edge of the mat to the animal fabric. On the back of the work, cut away the excess animal fabric, leaving only ¼in around the stitching line (**j**). Appliqué all 16 squares in the same way.

wrong side

Making up the quilt top

1 Lay the squares out in a pleasing way and sew them together in rows of four using ¼in seams (**k**); then join the rows together (**l**) to create the centre unit.

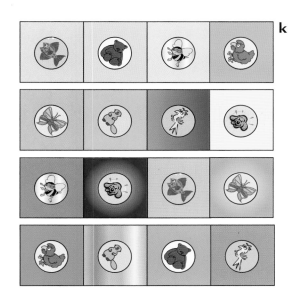

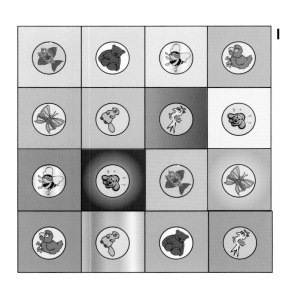

2 You're now going to IMA this complete unit to the background fabric as one piece. Paint a line of spray starch all around the unit ¼in in from the raw edge, and press a ¼in seam allowance over onto the freezer paper.

3 Tear a 30in square of background fabric and then place the square pieced unit on point in the centre of the background fabric (**m**). Pin it in place, then IMA it to the background fabric. Cut away the excess background fabric from behind the blocks, and remove the freezer paper shapes.

m

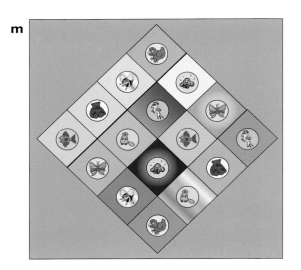

4 Tear four 5 x 40in strips of border fabric and sew them onto the four sides of the quilt (**n**), mitring the corners.

n

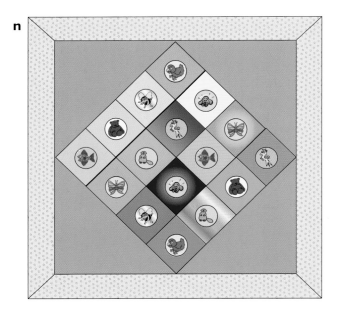

Quilting and finishing

1 Press the whole quilt top well, add your wadding and backing, and quilt. I stipple-quilted the blue background with YLI Machine Quilting Variegated thread. I also quilted in the ditch with invisible thread around the squares, and did a long curvy machine stitch every ½in in the border (below).

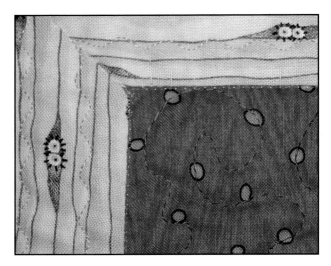

2 Bind the edges with 3½in strips folded in half (see pages 21-22), and then enjoy your peep-holes!

Template A
peep-hole
cut 1 from
template plastic

Drunkard's Path

Yes, it's time to head down that well-worn Drunkard's Path once again … In an effort to continue my campaign to help quilters to really *like* making Drunkard's Path quilts I'm offering more tips and ideas for making fabulous quilts using just one block!

In Book One I showed you how to make turtles with Drunkard's Path blocks, but what would you think about using up your scraps and setting them in this interesting layout (**a**)? This simple 16-block design would look great worked in scraps and tone-on-tone neutrals; the 12 Drunkard's Path blocks in the border set off the central pattern perfectly (**b**).

Or try using African fabrics as Kris Brown did in Scotland, for her quilt *Nairobi to Malindi* (above).

Imagine making very subtle DP blocks as a background, then appliquéing over them. Or, put four blocks together and you have a Snowball block. This can produce a very contemporary quilt using stunning hand-dyes and batiks (right). Try using various light, medium and dark fabrics in one colour to make this Snowball variation (**c**) with a super 'braided' border.

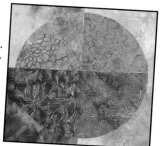

a

b

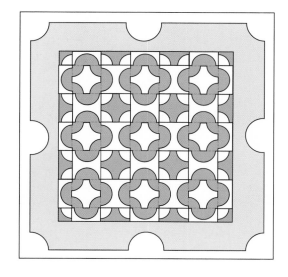

c

Phoenix Rising *2001*

You could use the curves to make a medallion border as I did in *Phoenix Rising* (above) – or as I call it, *Kermit The Frog In A Blender*. Even the centre pineapple blocks are IMAed onto the background. So much easier than sewing an inset seam, don't you agree?

Flip the Drunkard's Path blocks from *Phoenix Rising* (the layout shown in **d**) around a bit to create a slightly different look (**e**), and you could use the centre area for a stunning appliqué of your choice (IMA, of course!).

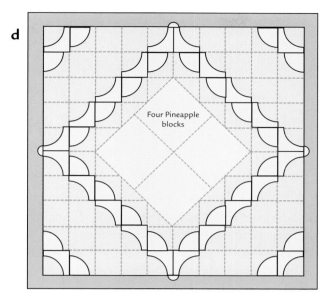

d — Four Pineapple blocks

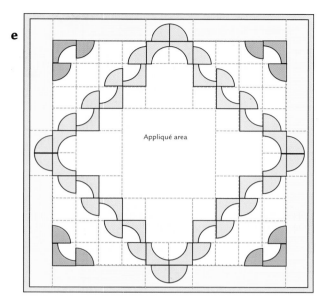

e — Appliqué area

Designing your own personal Drunkard's Path block

You can customize your own block, drawing it out to the exact size you choose, by following these simple directions:

1 On graph paper draw a square the ***finished size*** of the block you need (the red line on **a**).

2 Draw two dots about three quarters of the way along from the upper left-hand corner on two adjacent sides (**b**).

3 Using compasses, position the point in the corner and the pencil tip on the first dot. Draw around to the other dot (**c**).

4 Add a ¼in seam allowance to the two straight sides (**d**).

5 Use this shape to make a curved template from clear template plastic (**e**).

6 Cut your background square 1in larger in each direction than your original square (**f**) – that gives you ¼in seam allowance on each side of the square and room for the curve to 'float'.

Placing your dot closer to or further from the corner will result in different looks. Generally a good ratio is ⅔ for the DP quarter-circle to ⅓ background, but why not play around and see what happens?

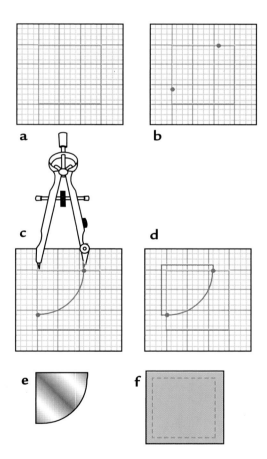

a

b

c

d

e

f

Draw a few different blocks on graph paper, photocopy them and allow yourself time to play with various layouts. Who knows what you might discover …

Fairy Frost

Often in workshops I suggest that students try working with
the Drunkard's Path design using only two colours.
'It would look stunning!' I say. But had I ever done it? No.

Then one day I was shown a new line from
Michael Miller Fabrics. Every colour was lovely,
and the fabric had a subtle, soft shimmer. It
was called ... wait for it ... Fairy Frost! I loved
it, and I immediately gravitated to my usual
autumnal colours. But then a friend's daughter
pointed out the crystal clear blue and the cold,
crisp white. I got the shivers! I saw a cold
winter morning in Colorado, the blue sky
making the clean, newly-fallen snow glisten.
I knew I had to make it.

So how can I tempt you? What about buying
that amazing batik you've been drooling over?
Or finally use that fabulous flower print you've
been hoarding? Choose a contrasting fabric
and you're on your way! Remember ... there
are only two blocks in this quilt, and it's easily
made with **IMA** and straight piecing.

Quilt dimensions: about 90 x 80in

You will need:

**For Drunkard's Path curves, the small
background squares, the border and
the binding**
❖ 8¼yd Colour 1 fabric (blue on my quilt)

**For Drunkard's Path curves and the large
background squares**
❖ 4yd Colour 2 fabric (white on my quilt)

For the backing
❖ 5¾yd (pieced)

Other requirements
❖ 90 x 80in wadding (I had my quilt top long-
arm machine quilted, and used Soft & Bright
by the Warm Company)
❖ 5m freezer paper
❖ spray starch and brush
❖ **threads:** YLI Wonder Invisible thread,
100% cotton thread to match your fabrics
(I used 60/2 in grey for piecing)

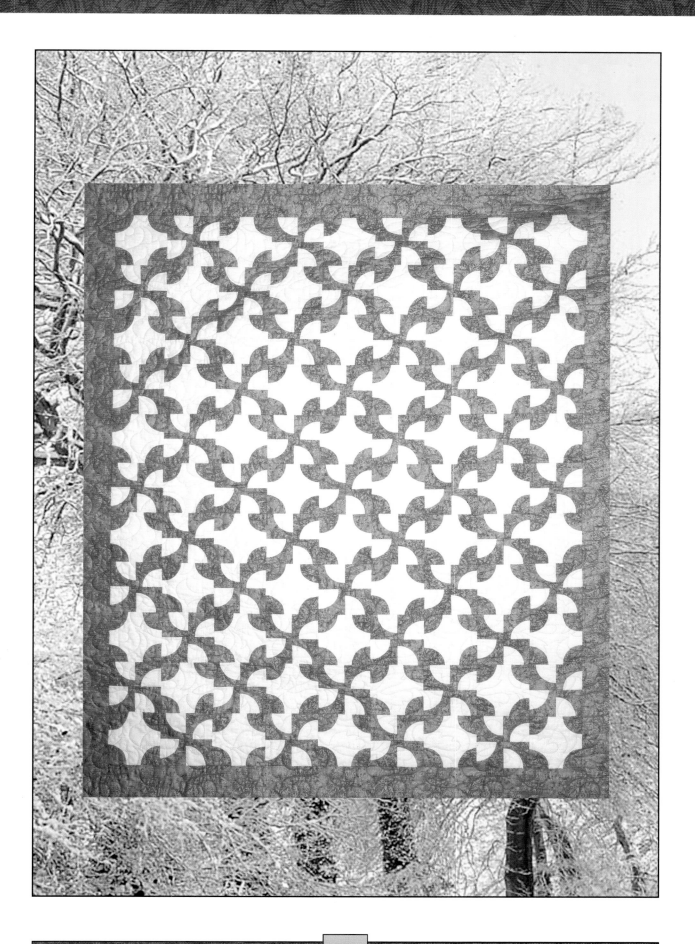

Preparation

From the length of Colour 1 fabric cut a 1yd length for the binding. From this piece cut:

– 10 3½in strips across the grain (this gives you strips 40in long)

From the remaining piece of Colour 1 fabric cut 2¾yd for the borders. From this piece, tear:

– 2 10¼ x 84in strips

– 2 10¼ x 95in strips

From the rest of the Colour 1 fabric, cut:

– 200 3¾in squares for the small background patches

– 50 7in squares for the large background patches

From Colour 2 fabric cut:

– 200 3in squares for the Drunkard's Path curves

– 50 7in squares for the inner curve shapes

Trace onto the freezer paper:

– 50 Drunkards Path curves (template **A**)

– 12 inner curve pieces (template **B**)

Cut all these shapes out. (You actually need 200 DP curves and 50 inner curve pieces but if you reuse them each four times you can save on time and freezer paper!)

Making the blocks

Use Method 1 (see page 36) throughout. To make the instructions easier, I'll use the term 'light' to describe where I've used the white fabric (Colour 2), and 'dark' where I've used the blue fabric (Colour 1).

1 Prepare 200 light DP curves using the freezer paper shapes and the 3in squares of light fabric (**a**). The template includes seam allowances on the straight sides, so you only need to press a seam allowance over the curved edge; cut the fabric patches even with the freezer paper template on the straight sides (**b**). IMA each light DP curve onto a 3¾in square of dark fabric (**c**).

2 Prepare 50 light inner curves using the freezer paper shapes and the 7in squares of light fabric (**d**). Once again, the template includes seam allowances on the straight sides: cut the fabric even with the straight edges, and only add and press over the seam allowance on the curved edges (**e**). IMA each light inner curve section onto a 7in square of dark fabric (**f**). (This makes a B block.)

3 On all the blocks, cut away the dark background fabric behind the light fabric, graduating the seams as shown by trimming the blue fabric closer to the seam and leaving the white seam allowance longer (**g**); you have IMAed a light fabric onto a dark background, and if you don't trim the seams this way there's a chance of a show-through.

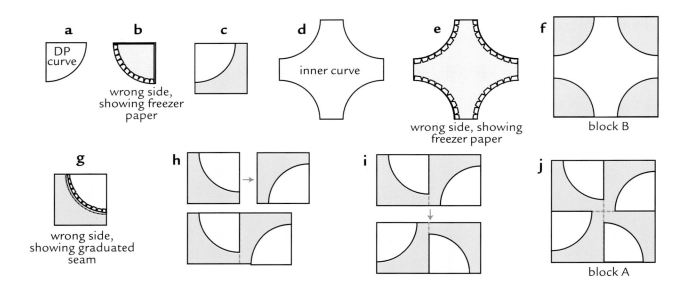

4 You'll now be joining sets of four small patches to create 50 four-patch A blocks. I found it easiest to do this by first creating 100 pairs of DP squares; the pairs must always look as shown in **h**. Press the seam down to the blue background. Flip half of the sets over (**i**) and sew two sets of pairs together to create an A block (**j**).

Creating the quilt top

1 There are eleven rows in this quilt. Row one has nine blocks joined as shown in **k**; row two has nine blocks joined as shown in **l**, and the other nine rows alternate these layouts. Press the seams of each row alternately so that they will match well when you're sewing the rows together; join all the rows in the correct order to create the central panel of the quilt top (**m**).

2 Sew on the borders and mitre the corners. Your quilt top is now complete.

Finishing

1 Layer your backing fabric, wadding and quilt top and quilt as you wish by hand or machine. Piece the binding strips together and use them to bind the edges of your quilt, following the instructions on page 20.

Could anything be easier? You could have made 200 light-on-dark blocks and 200 dark-on-light blocks but I realised that by using reverse appliqué to make an inner curve template you save having to sew 100 extra seams! It looks no different, and gives you time for a pint at the pub.

Dr Cathy Corbishley made the birds in flight (below) using just two colours, and saved so much time that she could invest hours in machine quilting that is positively a dream to behold!

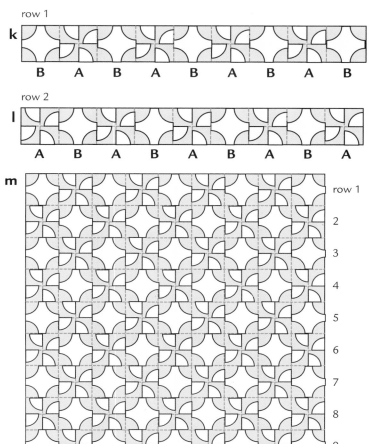

row 1

k

B A B A B A B A B

row 2

l

A B A B A B A B A

m

row 1
2
3
4
5
6
7
8
9
10
11

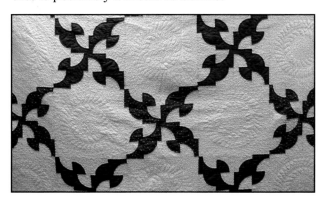

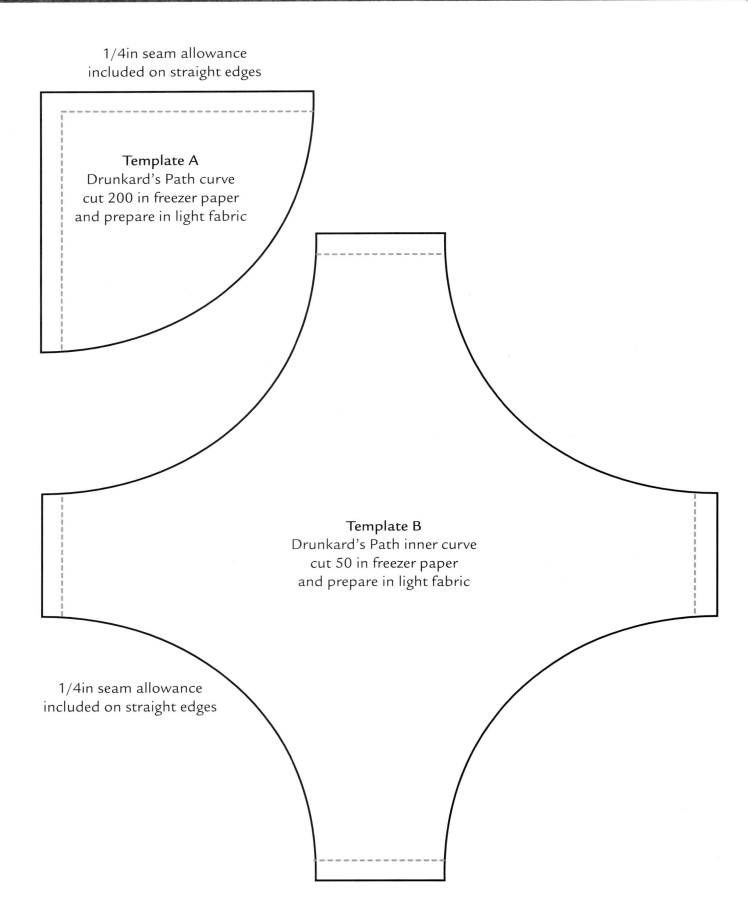

1/4in seam allowance
included on straight edges

Template A
Drunkard's Path curve
cut 200 in freezer paper
and prepare in light fabric

Template B
Drunkard's Path inner curve
cut 50 in freezer paper
and prepare in light fabric

1/4in seam allowance
included on straight edges

Making Braided Handles and Stems

Anytime I can add dimension to my work I do; it enhances that tactile feel that I love in quilts. Why make a simple flat handle for a basket when you can easily plait three stems and make a super braided handle? For easy ways to make bias stems see page 33.

Making bias handles

1 Pin the end of each bias tube or folded strip securely to your ironing board, edges touching (**a**).

2 Cross the far right tube over the centre one (**b**), then cross the far left tube over the centre one. Come on now ... you all know how to plait/braid! Keep the braid flat and loose as you work (**c**); continue plaiting to the end of the tubes.

3 Hand-stitch the loose ends together so that the plait can't unbraid (**d**). You'll find that the plait easily bends into a handle shape (**e**).

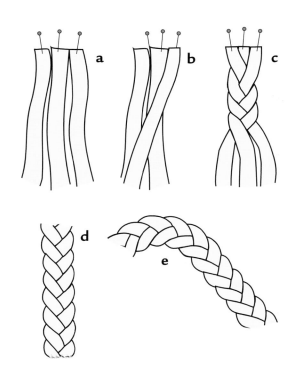

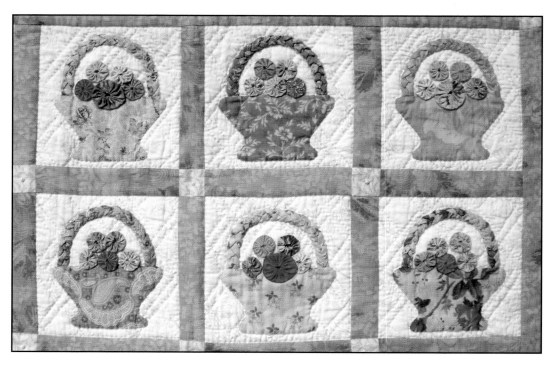

Aunt Helen's Baskets

This quilt is dedicated to my Aunt Helen Lewandowski (1907-1998).
My grandparents died before I was born, so she and my Uncle Roman
filled that generation's role in my life. Aunt Helen was a lovely,
nurturing woman, who lived a simple life in a house my uncle built with
his own hands in the North Woods of Wisconsin. I always see her, in her pinny,
standing by her wood cooking-stove, a smile on her face. With her light hair
and clear blue eyes she was a timeless lady, soft-spoken and kind,
who seemed to come from a gentler, bygone era.

Aunt Helen was the only other quilter in my family, but we only found her quilts after her death. Although she was gone I wanted to create a lasting link between us and so I made this quilt for her. Now, whenever I show this quilt at lectures I know she is sitting up there in quilting heaven, looking down on me and thinking 'How nice!' I'm sure she likes the tactile, braided handles and the Suffolk Puff (yoyo) flowers with their pearl centres. The meandering vine border and scalloped frame are all easily worked in **IMA** to create this soft and nostalgic quilt. Make the bias strips for the trailing vine using Aunt Helen's own method, or use a Clover bias maker (see page 33).

ABOVE: *Aunt Helen aged 21*

RIGHT: *Aunt Helen and me, Christmas 1961,
getting the Christmas tree in Eagle River, Wisconsin*

Quilt dimensions: 55 x 60in

You will need:

For the block backgrounds and the first border
❖ 1⅞yd neutral-coloured fabric

For the sashing
❖ ½yd green fabric 1

For the border
❖ 1¾yd green fabric 2

For the binding
❖ ⅝yd green fabric (use either of your green fabrics for the binding)
❖ ¼yd pink fabric for the inset strip

For the baskets (there are 20 in the quilt)
❖ 20 different fabrics, one 12in square of each

For the border appliqué and the flowers
❖ 100in of green bias binding ¼in wide
❖ enough scraps of green fabric for 40 leaves
❖ assorted plain and print fabrics in a variety of colours for the flowers
❖ tiny pearls if you wish to embellish your flowers

Other requirements
❖ 2½yd freezer paper (for baskets and scalloped border)
❖ spray starch and brush
❖ 3yd backing fabric (if pieced horizontally)
❖ 55 x 60in wadding (I used thin polyester wadding)
❖ **threads:** 100% cotton for piecing, YLI Wonder Invisible for IMA, YLI Hand Quilting, and YLI silk thread for stipple-quilting the final border

Preparation

Begin by tearing lengthwise strips for your borders.

From the neutral background fabric tear:
– two 45 x 7in strips
– two 50 x 7in strips

From the green border fabric tear:

– two 60 x 8½in strips
– two 65 x 8½in strips

From the remaining green fabric cut:
– six 1½ x 40in strips – then subcut these into thirty-one 1½ x 6in strips for the sashing
– two 1½ x 25in strips for top and bottom sashings
– two 1½ x 32in strips for side sashings
– seven 3 x 40in strips for the binding

From the yellow fabric cut:
– one 1½ x 40in strip – then subcut this into sixteen 1½in squares

Set all these strips safely to one side for the moment.

Creating the basket blocks

1 Use a rotary cutter to cut twenty 6in square blocks of background fabric.

2 Lay the freezer paper over the basket template (**A** on page 74); trace and cut out 20 basket shapes from the freezer paper.

3 You'll now be using each 12in square of basket fabric to create bias strips and a basket shape, as shown (**a**). From every square cut three bias strips, each 1¼in wide; each strip must be at least 6in long. Use these to make folded bias strips; I made mine by using the Clover bias maker. Press one freezer paper basket shape onto the reverse side of the remaining piece of fabric; prepare the shapes for IMA using method 1 (see page 36). You now have 20 different basket shapes ready to appliqué (**b**).

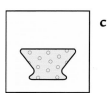

4 Follow the instructions on page 67 to make the bias strips up into plaited handles for the baskets.

5 Place one prepared basket shape in position on one square of background fabric (**c**). Slip the ends of the matching braided handle underneath the top edge, just in from each side (**d**); pin in position if necessary to prevent them from slipping.

6 IMA the whole design in position, stitching round the basket shape and round the inside and outside edges of the handle. You'll easily be able to stitch over the braided ends. (It's **not** too thick … just stitch slowly!)

7 Prepare the remaining basket blocks in the same way.

Adding the sashing

1 Lay the basket blocks out in five rows of four blocks. Stitch a green sashing strip into each gap between the blocks, so that you have five rows that look as shown in **e**.

e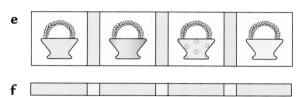

f

2 Make a row of four green sashing strips interspersed with three yellow squares (**f**). Make three more sashing rows in the same way.

3 Stitch alternate sashing and basket rows together as shown (**g**) to create the centre of the quilt top, pressing all seams towards the sashing throughout.

g

4 Sew one yellow square onto each end of both 1½ x 25in sashing strips (**h**). Sew one 1½ x 32in green strip to each side of the basket unit (**i**); then attach the strips with the yellow corners to the top and bottom edges of the basket unit (**j**). The centre of the quilt top is now complete.

h

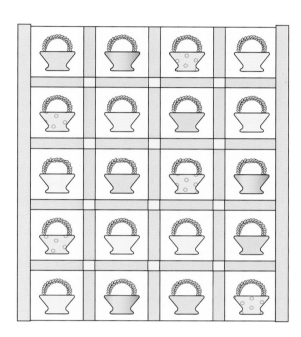

i

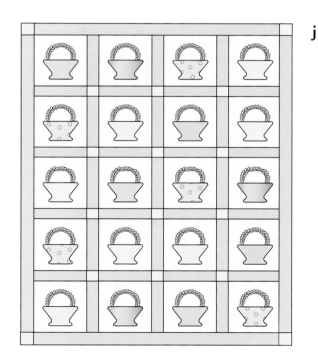

j

Making the flowers

1 Use template **B** to cut 44 circles of assorted fabrics for the flowers, and template **C** to cut 80 smaller circles. To make a puff, turn under a very fine hem around the circle of fabric as you sew a running stitch around the turned-under edge (**k**). Once you've sewn all the way around, pull your thread tight to draw the circle into a puff (**l**), then knot the thread off securely. Use the point of your needle to coax the puff into a nice shape. The first ones may slightly resemble a mis-shapen fried egg, but they will get better!

2 Make flowers out of all the fabric circles and stab-stitch a selection of puffs in place on each basket (**m**); I used one large flower in almost every basket, along with several small ones, but some baskets contain only five small flowers … it really depends on how the mood takes you. Save the remaining large flowers for decorating the border appliqué – I used only large flowers on the border, but again you could use a mixture. I also put artificial pearls into the centres of the large flowers.

I guess it's now time to come clean. I didn't make the puffs for my baskets: my mother Lorraine did! She is an absolute expert in making yoyos, and who was I to deny her the pleasure? She also made the puffs for *Try To Remember* … (see page 107).

If you're not too fond of making Suffolk Puffs, you could fill the baskets with pretty buttons or appliqué some other flowers. There's also nothing wrong with stencilling flowers – or leaving the baskets empty!

Making the appliqué border

1 On large sheets of paper, draw up the scalloped border templates (**D** and **E**) on page 75 to the correct size. (Don't worry too much about the exact depth of the scallops; just make sure that the curves are nice and smooth and even.) Lay the template pieces on the neutral fabric strips and check their sizes against the central panel (remember to leave space for the trailing vine design); if necessary, increase or decrease the length of the templates slightly by adjusting the centres. Trace the complete shapes onto freezer paper twice each.

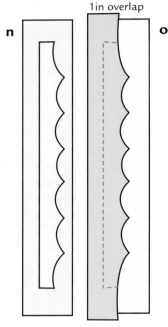

2 Cut out the freezer paper templates and iron one onto the reverse side of each green border strip (**n**). Prepare the scalloped edge of each shape using Method 1 (see page 36) and I**MA** the scalloped edge of each shape onto one of the strips of neutral fabric (**o**); the shapes will overlap the neutral fabric by about 1in. Remove the freezer paper.

3 Sew the scalloped borders onto the body of the quilt. Mitre the corners using I**MA** (**p**).

4 Trace the leaf templates (**F**) onto freezer paper 40 times, then cut these shapes out and use spray starch to prepare them for appliquéing.

5 Make a 100in length of ¼in finished bias tape using your favourite method. When you position the trailing vine design around the neutral part of the border, keep it casual; you don't

want the curves to look too mathematical. Use the diagram (*above*) to show you roughly how the vine stem and leaves fit in around the scallops. IMA the stems and leaves in place; I've joined the stems under the flower shapes when necessary. Remove the freezer paper shapes behind the leaves.

6 Use the stab stitch to stitch the flowers on the vine as shown (**q**). Add tiny pearls if you wish.

q

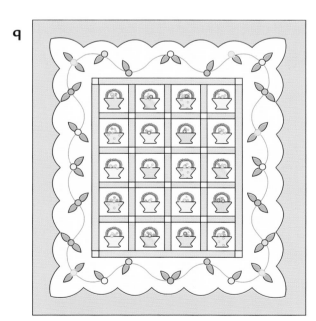

Finishing

1 Layer your background fabric, wadding and quilt top, then quilt as you wish by hand or machine. I hand quilted the white background with a double cross-hatching which I felt looked like a garden trellis. The green final border is machine quilted in vermicelli/stipple quilting. Bind the edges to finish your quilt, following the instructions on page 22 for adding folded insert strips of the pink fabric.

2 If you've read Book One, you may remember seeing the label I made for this quilt (on page 41), using Aunt Helen's engagement photo. Don't forget to make a lovely label for your basket quilt!

I did my machine stipple quilting using YLI silk thread, with 60wt in the bobbin to match the backing, and a 60/10 Denim/Jeans needle. This thread performed beautifully, it feels heavenly, and was definitely worth the slightly higher price of the thread compared with cotton. Why not try it?

Hollis, Aunt Helen and Rachel, 1986, the last time we saw her ...

Template B
large flower
cut 44 shapes from
assorted fabrics

Template C
small flower
cut 80 shapes from
assorted fabrics

dotted lines
show position
of handles

Template A
basket
cut 20 shapes from
freezer paper

Template F
leaf
cut 40 shapes from
freezer paper and
prepare in green fabric

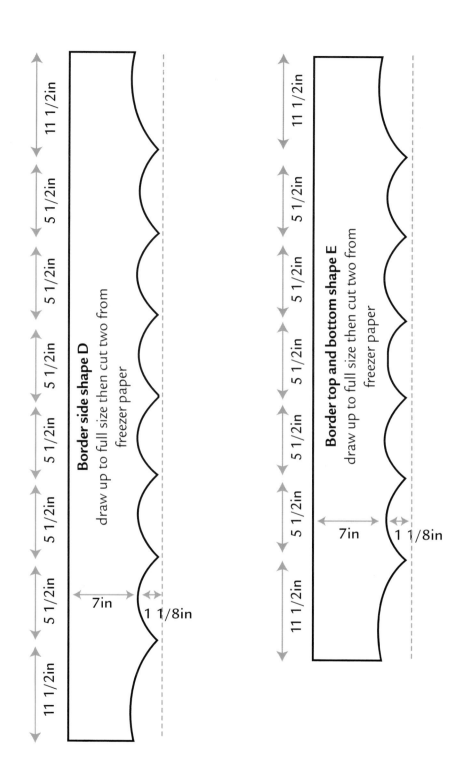

Border side shape D
draw up to full size then cut two from freezer paper

11 1/2in · 5 1/2in · 5 1/2in · 5 1/2in · 5 1/2in · 5 1/2in · 5 1/2in · 5 1/2in · 11 1/2in

7in 1 1/8in

Border top and bottom shape E
draw up to full size then cut two from freezer paper

11 1/2in · 5 1/2in · 5 1/2in · 5 1/2in · 5 1/2in · 5 1/2in · 11 1/2in

7in 1 1/8in

Appliqué Over Pieced Blocks

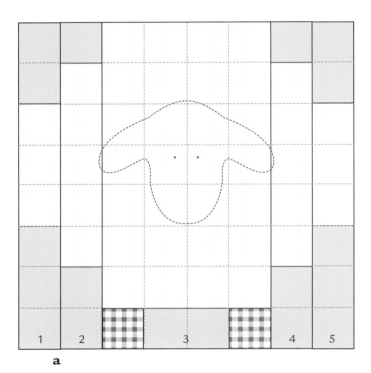

a

My sheep Gorse *and* Babe

Sometimes you may want to do your appliqué over a pieced design or a pieced background. Even though you'll have to stitch over bulky seams, there's no problem when you're using IMA; just pretend that you're IMAing on a plain background and be careful when you cut the pieced background away.

I was in Scotland teaching during the outbreak of Foot & Mouth disease a few years ago. Every time I drove past a flock of unaffected sheep I'd roll down my window and shout, 'RUN! Run north! And don't inhale!' Unfailingly they just stood there and watched me blankly. When I returned home I knew I had to immortalize them. After several drawings I realized that ordinary appliqué just didn't seem to work, so I pieced them using IMA only for the faces.

Making a sheep block

Each sheep block is created from five strips. Diagram **a** shows a finished block, and you can see how the different sections of the block are broken down based on a 1in grid.

Rows 1 and 5 are made of a 2in strip of grass, a 3in strip of sheep fleece, and a 3in strip of grass.

Rows 2 and 4 are made from a 1in strip of grass, a 5in strip of sheep fleece, and a 2in strip of grass.

Row 3 is 4in wide, and made from a 7 x 4in rectangle, two 1in square feet, and a 1 x 2in grass strip.

Remember that all these measurements are **finished** size. I suggest that you cut numerous strips of grass and fleece fabric and then cut each piece to the correct length; this way you can use lots of different neutrals for the fleeces if you wish.

From green fabric cut:
    five pieces 1½ x 2½in (A-E)
    two pieces 1½ x 3½in (F and G)
    two pieces 1½ x 1½in (H and I)

From fleece fabric cut:
    two pieces 1½ x 3½in (J and K)
    two pieces 1½ x 5½in (L and M)
    one piece 4½ x 7½in (N)

From leg fabric cut:
    two pieces 1½ x 1½in (O and P)

Follow the sequence shown (**b-d**) to piece each block, and press all the seams to the grass when possible. Trace the sheep head shape (template **A**) onto freezer paper the required number of times, and use Method 1 (see page 36) to prepare the head shapes from the plaid fabrics (**e**). IMA a head in place on each block (**f**). Tweak each face in a slightly different direction so that each sheep has a personality of its own, and add two little black beads for eyes (**g**). If you like, add a tail to one sheep who's heading home (see photograph below)!

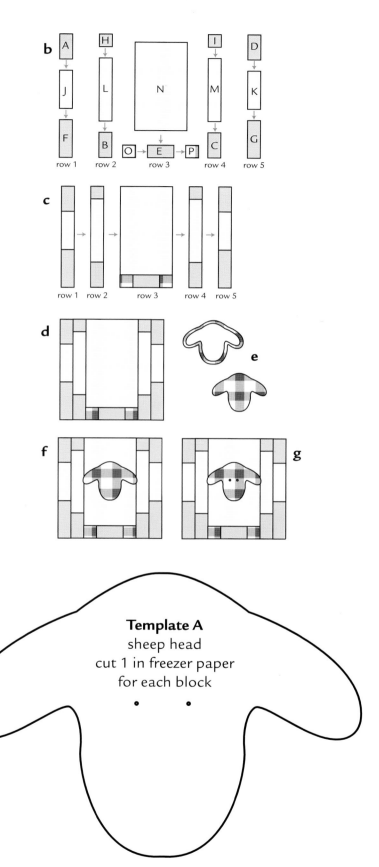

Template A
sheep head
cut 1 in freezer paper
for each block

Sheep On My Hills

A collection of sheep blocks pieced into a central panel, plus an IMAed sun and hills, creates a flock of sheep grazing in the countryside. As these are Scottish sheep they have plaid faces and a tartan border. The wee doggies are foundation-paper-pieced from the book *A Quilter's Ark* by Margaret Rolfe (published by That Patchwork Place). I also used IMA to provide a solution for a tricky, mis-matched border. Mitring was never easier!

This would be a great quilt for a hard-to-please young boy, your neighbour the sheep farmer, or for yourself. Increase or decrease the numbers in the flock to make just the size you want.

Quilt dimensions: 84 x 89in
(using 25 8in finished sheep blocks)

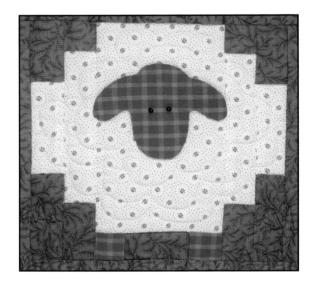

For the full-size quilt you will need:

For the sky
❖ 60 x 16in 'sky-looking' fabric

For the grass and sashing
❖ 3yd green fabric

For the sheeps' fleeces
❖ 1½yd tone-on-tone white (or an assortment of neutrals, one 8in square for each sheep)

For the faces and legs
❖ one 8in square of tartan/plaid for each sheep

For the sun
❖ ¼yd yellow fabric

For the dogs (optional)
❖ scraps of black and white fabric

For the border
❖ I used 60in-wide tartan fabric and tore the border strips 12in wide; if you use 44in-wide fabric you'd make better use of it by tearing the border 10½in wide from 3yd of fabric

For the binding
❖ 8 strips 3½in wide (the precise yardage will depend on your fabric's width)

For the backing
❖ 5yd

Other requirements
❖ 84 x 89in wadding
❖ 50 tiny black seed beads for the sheeps' eyes
❖ 4yd freezer paper (most of this is for the hills)
❖ spray starch and brush
❖ greaseproof paper and iron-on interfacing for the sun
❖ **threads:** 100% cotton for piecing, YLI Wonder Invisible for IMA, and your own choice of threads for hand or machine quilting

Preparation

From the green fabric cut ten 1½ x 40in strips, selvedge to selvedge. Sub-cut these as follows:

- for the vertical sashing strips between the sheep blocks, sub-cut five of the strips into 20 strips each 1½ x 8½in

- for the horizontal strips between rows, piece the other five strips together and then sub-cut them into strips 1½ x 44½in

Follow the instructions on page 76 to create 25 sheep blocks.

Making the quilt

1 Each row of the centre panel consists of five sheep blocks separated by vertical sashing strips (**a**). Once you've created five rows in this way, join the rows with a horizontal sashing strip between them (**b**).

a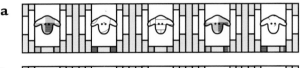

b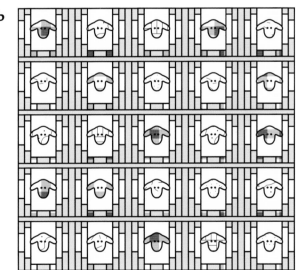

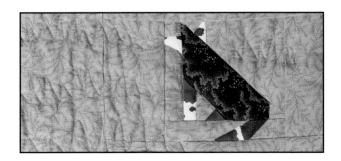

2 Tear three strips of grass fabric, each 8½ x 44½in, and sew one to each side of the pieced centre panel (**c**). If you're adding the dogs, follow the instructions in the book to paper-piece them and add strips to bring the panels up to 8½in, to match the width of the borders. Sew one dog on each side of the remaining grass strip and sew this unit onto the bottom of the centre panel (**d**). (If you're not adding the dogs, simply make your third strip 8½ x 60½in and add it to the bottom in the usual way.)

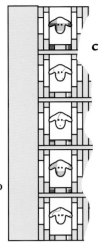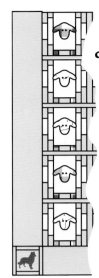

3 For the sky, tear a strip of sky fabric 16½ x 60½in. Cut a strip of freezer paper the same size and draw your hills free-form. Now don't go all strange on me! Just draw hills … they're only curves after all! Do remember, though, that they will be **reversed** once you IMA them.

4 Foundation-piece the sun's rays using template **B** traced onto greaseproof paper; if you're not sure how to do the foundation piecing, follow the instructions on page 94. Use yellow for the inner points, and the sky fabric for the outer points. I used iron-on interfacing for turning the curve of the points (see page 38). Use freezer paper and spray starch (see page 36) for the sun centre, working with template **C**. IMA the sun centre onto the ray section, then IMA the sun onto the upper right-hand side of the sky (**e**). Prepare and IMA the hills, and piece this unit onto the top of the quilt (**f**).

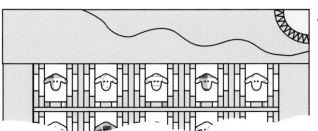

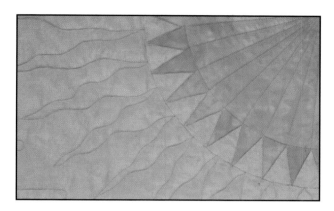

Not into sheep? How about a Highland cow?

5 Measure the quilt and tear your tartan border strips to fit (see the fabric requirements for hints on tearing these). Add these to the quilt top, setting the corners square or mitring. As I used a tartan fabric, I knew that the mitres would never match. I debated about putting some contrasting square in the corner but I wanted the sheep to get all the attention, and a busy border would detract from them. So ... once again **IMA** came to the rescue! I cut a 1¼ x 16in strip of the tartan for each

corner. I pressed ¼in in on each side and on the bottom. I spray-starched them and then **IMA**ed them over the awkward match on the mitre (**g**)! It worked a treat and I think it actually looks better then if the plaid had matched ... What is life but a series of inspired follies?

6 Layer, quilt and bind your quilt top to complete the project (**h**).

If sheep are not your thing, try replacing them with Highland cows: the pattern is below. Use template **D** for the head, **E** for the horns, **F** for the nose and **G** for the fringe. If you work on a 1in grid for this design, the block comes out larger than the sheep (10in rather than 8in square), so just set them 4 x 4 and cut your sashing strips 10½ x 1½in.

From green fabric cut:
 two pieces 2 x 10½in (A and B)
 two pieces 2 x 2½in (C and D)
 one piece 2½ x 4½in (E)
 two pieces 2 x 3½in (F and G)
 one piece 2½in square (H)
 two pieces 1 x 1½in (I and J)

From fleece fabric cut:
 two pieces 2 x 5½in (K and M)
 one piece 4½ x 6½in (L)

From leg fabric cut:
 two pieces 1½ x 2in (N and O)

Highland cow pattern

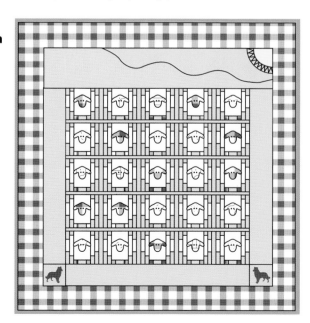

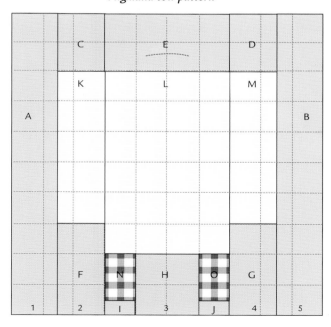

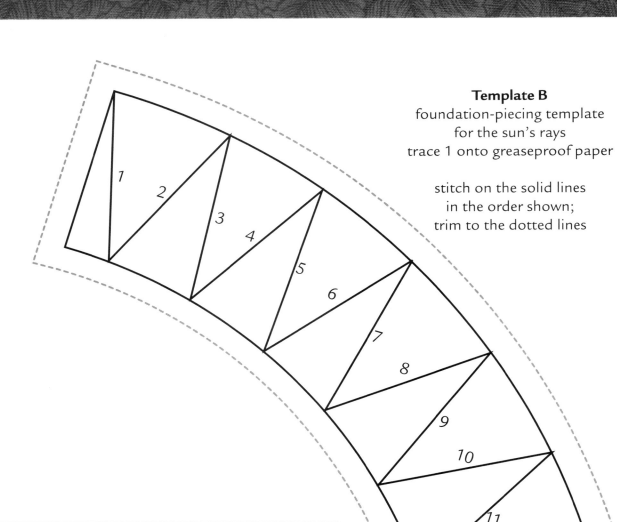

Template B
foundation-piecing template
for the sun's rays
trace 1 onto greaseproof paper

stitch on the solid lines
in the order shown;
trim to the dotted lines

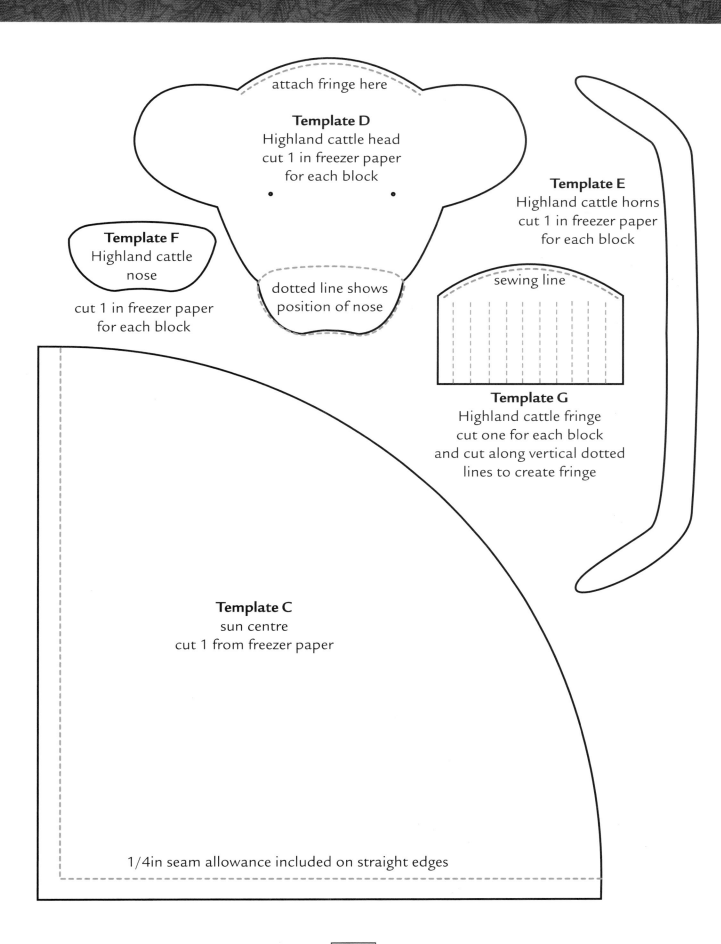

attach fringe here

Template D
Highland cattle head
cut 1 in freezer paper
for each block

Template E
Highland cattle horns
cut 1 in freezer paper
for each block

Template F
Highland cattle
nose

cut 1 in freezer paper
for each block

dotted line shows
position of nose

sewing line

Template G
Highland cattle fringe
cut one for each block
and cut along vertical dotted
lines to create fringe

Template C
sun centre
cut 1 from freezer paper

1/4in seam allowance included on straight edges

Appli-Piecing Hexagons

It was embarrassing to admit that I'd been making quilts for over 30 years and still had not made a hexagon quilt. I guess that was because repetition is not my strong point, and all that preparation sounded as though it would be terribly dull. But I wanted sunflowers for *Geese in my Garden*, and hexagons seemed the best way to produce them.

Hand piecing wasn't an option once I realised that I could piece them by appliquéing them to each other. IMA with the blind hem stitch didn't work, but a long, narrow zigzag did the trick. Freezer paper and spray starch made the preparation work fast, and soon I was producing flowers by the handful! **And** they were fun to make. You could also use this same technique for piecing Dresden Plates or Attic Windows if you like – construct your unit with the zigzag and then IMA it onto your background.

Making a hexagon flower

1 For each flower, trace template **A** onto freezer paper seven times, then cut the hexagons out. Iron the hexagons onto the wrong side of your flower fabric; I used the same fabric for the outside petals, and a different fabric for the centres to make them look more like flowers. Prepare these hexagons using Method 1 (page 36). You now have six 'petal' hexagons and one 'flower centre' hexagon (**a**).

2 Lay the hexagons out in the flower shape and set your machine up for IMA. **But**, instead of using the blind hem stitch we will use an open narrow zigzag (**b**) for the appli-piecing.

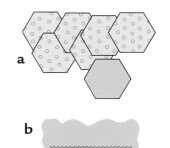

Begin stitching at the outside of the shape, and zigzag down two sides of the hexagon in a reverse 'L' shape (**c**). Continue around the shape in the same way (**d**) to create a complete flower (**e**).

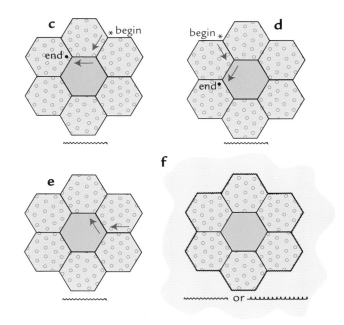

3 Once all the hexagons have been appli-pieced you can position the flower on your quilt and do traditional IMA (blind hem or buttonhole) on the outside edge (**f**). Cut away the background fabric on the reverse of the work and remove the freezer paper shapes. You could make a complete quilt of these hexagons using appli-piecing, and then IMA it onto your borders so you have a straight-edged quilt and don't have the problem of binding a multi-edged quilt!

One of the most talented, creative, giving and modest ladies I know is Paula Doyle, who owns Green Mountain Quilts in Staines, just west of London. She kindly suggested an alternative layout for flowers using an elongated hexagon for the petals, and an octagon for the flower centres (**g**).

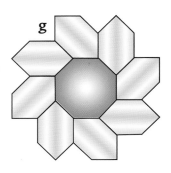

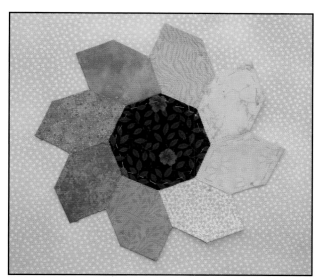

Paula flower: finishes at 6½in

You could replace your hexagon flowers with Paula's flowers, using template **B** for the petals and template **C** for the flower centres, or mix the two! If you want to create an overall design using Paula flowers, you'll also need to add a small square (template **D**) where shown to make the tesselations work (**h**).

Paula also offered this helpful hint: when you begin and end your zigzag appli-piecing, try dropping your feed dogs for the first few stitches. This locks the stitches without having to reduce your stitch length.

Diagrams **i** and **j** show two other flower designs created from five-sided petal shapes; use templates **E** and **F** if you fancy trying these designs.

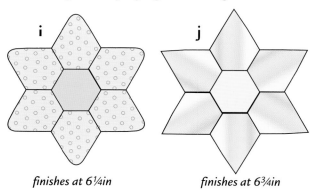

finishes at 6¼in   *finishes at 6¾in*

Template A
flower petal and centre
cut 7 for each
flower from
freezer paper

Template D
square filler
template

Template B
alternative petal
cut 8 of these from
freezer paper
for each
flower

Template F
alternative petal
cut 6 of these and
1 hexagon from
freezer paper
for each
flower

Template E
alternative petal
cut 6 of these and
1 hexagon from
freezer paper
for each
flower

Template C
octagon flower centre
cut 1 of these from
freezer paper for
each flower

Geese In The Garden

For several years after they retired my parents came to live with us in our home near Tunbridge Wells. Every summer we would plant sunflowers in their garden, and when they moved to Florida recently I wanted to make a quilt with the biggest sunflowers ever! And as I had never made hexagons in over 30 years of quiltmaking I thought it was high time to give them a go. Hand piecing them was a definite non-starter, and so they're all 'appli-pieced' with IMA.

Geese In The Garden is basically a 'strippy quilt', with all stems, leaves, flowers and geese done in traditional IMA. I actually had two geese who resided with me as lawn mowers. They were lovely geese but, as geese tend to, they looked rather similar. So when it came time to name them I decided it was best to name them after the two characters in *The Christmas Carol*, Marley and Marley. This way, no matter who I spoke to, I always got their name right!

The quilt was first named *Geese In The Garden* because of the Flying Geese strips. But on the day I planned to tack the quilt I first went out to say hi to my two friends, and couldn't find them. A search of the orchard resulted in my finding the torn bodies of the Marleys, who had been murdered by foxes the night before. I was devastated. After seeing to their remains I went back to my quilt and decided it needed real geese, so my two lovely Marleys live on forever on their quilt.

I invite you to use them on your quilt. Remember, the one at the top is Marley ... no the one at the bottom is Marley. Marley is on top!

You can also make the quilt lap size (57in x 66in, as shown left); this is the size we do in my week-long workshops. I've taught it in France and in Spain, and on page 88 are some of the wonderful, creative results! Pick a colour theme and let your creative juices go wild.

The results of a week's workshop at the 'Spanish Experience' in the mountains outside Valencia (left) ... and from the same workshop in France (above) using Paula flowers!

Quilt dimensions: 82 x 88in

For the full-size quilt you will need:

For the appliqué strips

- ½yd green fabric for the bias strips (stems)
- 2½yd of freezer paper
- 12in squares of five different green fabrics for the leaves and ground
- scraps of assorted coloured fabrics for the flowers (each hexagon uses about 2½in square)
- 1½yd of background fabric. My quilt uses heaps of different 'tone-on-tone' fabrics that together equal about 1½yd; strips are cut 8½ x 54in.

For the Flying Geese strips

- roughly 1¼yd coloured fabric for the geese (I used lots of scraps for my geese, but you could use all one fabric if you prefer; there are 27 geese in each strip plus one at the top and one at the bottom, so 29 in total)
- roughly 1½yd background fabric (again, the backgrounds on my strips are pieced from assorted scraps)
- five 5 x 55in strips of greaseproof (not geese-proof!) paper or tracing paper, if you wish to foundation-piece the flying geese strips

For the first border

- ¼yd (needs to be pieced)

For the second border

- 1yd (pieced)

For the final border

- 2½yd (torn on the lengthwise grain)

For the binding

- 1¼yd fabric, cut into strips along the straight grain

For the Marleys

- If you'll be asking Marley and Marley to join your quilt you will need a fat quarter of suitable goose fabric and scraps of gold for their feet and beaks, plus freezer paper

Other requirements

- 82 x 88in wadding (I used Mountain Mist Quilt-Light polyester bonded wadding)
- **threads:** 100% cotton for piecing, YLI Wonder Invisible for IMA, YLI Hand Quilting
- spray starch and brush

Making the appliquéd strips

1 Cut four 8½ x 54½in strips of background fabric to go behind the flowers (or piece scraps to equal these measurements).

2 Cut 1in strips of bias from the green fabric and piece them together to make four 55in lengths. Use Aunt Helen's method or Clover Bias stem makers (see page 33) to turn under the edges so that the binding finishes ½in wide.

3 Trace 20 leaf shapes (template **G**) and 4 ground pieces (template **H**) onto freezer paper, then cut these out and use Method 1 (see page 36) to prepare the shapes in the green fabrics (**a**).

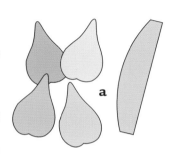

a

4 Trace 140 hexagon shapes onto freezer paper (you can get 7 hexagons from 2in of freezer paper), then cut these out and use Method 1 to prepare 120 flower petals and 20 contrasting flower centres in fabric. Use these shapes to appli-piece 20 hexagon flowers (see page 84) (**b**).

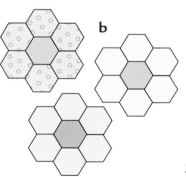

b

Sue Prins, who attended a class of mine in Cape Town, South Africa, shared a tip she learned from Francis Deacon of George, SA. When you press the fabric up and over onto the freezer paper make sure that your seam allowances all go in the same direction. We don't know why, but it really does provide a better fit when putting your hexagons together!

5 Position one bias stem on a background strip and curve it into a pleasing shape: IMA it in place (**c**). Position five prepared leaves on the outside curves of the stem as shown, and IMA them in place (**d**).

6 Position five of the pieced flowers in the spaces inside the curves of the stem, and IMA them in place (**e**). IMA a ground piece at the base of the stem (**f**). Appliqué the other three strips in the same way.

c   d   e   f

7 Remove all the freezer paper shapes from behind the flowers and leaves (see page 39), then embellish the centres of the flowers with beads or embroidery if you wish. Your appliqué strips are now finished; set them aside and proceed to the Flying Geese strips.

Piecing the Flying Geese strips

g

1 I used foundation paper piecing to make my flying geese strips; you could use any of the many good methods available, depending on your own preference. If you choose to foundation-piece with paper, use pencil to trace repeats of template **I** onto the paper strips so that you have 27 geese flying in a row on each strip (**g**). It's also possible to buy pre-printed rolls of flying geese strips; you will need strips that come out at a finished size of 4in wide x 2in tall.

2 Cut 161 3in squares of background fabric. Cut each square in half diagonally once; you now have 322 *half square triangles* (**h**).

h   straight edge   bias edge   straight edge   straight edge

3 Cut 41 5½in squares of your geese fabric(s). Cut each square in half diagonally twice. You now have 164 *quarter square triangle* geese (**i**); you'll be using 161 for your piecing.

i

4 To foundation-piece these geese, lay one large 'goose' triangle over the large bottom triangle on the reverse side of the paper. Hold it up to the light for correct positioning, and pin in place (**j**). Place the long edge of the background half square triangle over the goose, right sides together, and match the raw edges; pin (**k**). Flip to the reverse side and sew along the marked line (**l**). On the right side, flip up the triangle and press (**m**); repeat with the other background side (**n**).

j

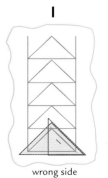

right side of
goose tracing   wrong side

k

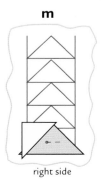

right side   wrong side

l   **m**   **n**

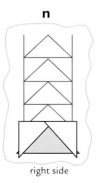

wrong side   right side   right side

o   **p**   **q**

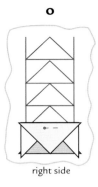 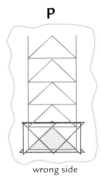

right side   wrong side   right side

r

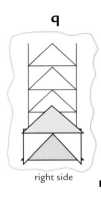

5 Place the next goose right sides together over the unit just sewn (**o**), pin, flip over the paper and sew on the dotted line (**p**). Press your goose up into position (**q**) and repeat steps i-q until your strip is full of flying geese (**r**); there are 27 geese in each strip. Then make two horizontal rows of 13 individual geese for the top and bottom (**s**); press well and remove the paper.

s

You may want to use a 60/2 thread for the foundation seams as the thinner thread reduces the bulk in the seams. Also, try reducing your stitch length to make it easier to remove the paper.

Making the quilt top

1 Piece the Flying Geese strips to the appliquéd strips (**t**) and press.

t

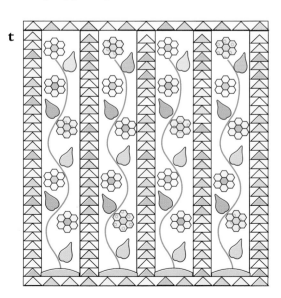

2 For border 1:

– tear two 1½ x 58½in strips, and sew these onto the sides of quilt.

– tear two 1½ x 54½in strips, and sew these to the top and bottom of quilt to complete the first border (**u**). Press the seams towards the border.

u

v

3 For border 2:

– tear two 4½ x 54½in strips, and sew these to the top and bottom of the quilt.

– tear two 4½ x 66½in strips, and sew these onto the sides of the quilt. You now have two borders round the central panel (**v**).

These two borders were straight-set and not mitred because of the fabric I chose. I did mitre my final border, though. Use these measurements as a guide and do what works best for your fabric choices.

4 For border 3:

– tear two 10½ x 85in strips along the lengthwise grain for the top and bottom.

– tear two 10½ x 90in strips along the lengthwise grain for the sides.

Add these strips to the quilt, either straight set or mitred, to complete the piecing (**w**).

w

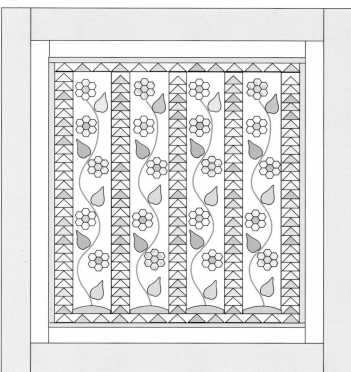

Adding the Marleys

1 Enlarge the drawings of the Marleys so that they are roughly 14in tall, then trace the different parts onto freezer paper. Prepare the bodies, beaks and feet using Method 1 and IMA them in the bottom left corner of the quilt (**x**). As I wanted my guys to be a bit fluffy, I placed a layer of thin polyester wadding under their bodies before I IMAed them – not too thick, and none under the beaks or feet. Sew on beads for eyes.

Finishing

My quilt was hand quilted. I planned to begin the quilting the day my daughter Hollis brought her newborn daughter Anastasia from Colorado to visit me. It was September 11, 2001, and I'd imagined hours of chatting while Hollis tended little A and I quilted. Instead we sat, as I'm sure you did, glued to our seats as we watched the horrific events unfold before our disbelieving eyes. I quilted, she nursed, but we didn't chat much that day. So *Geese In The Garden* is a bit of a sad quilt: parents leaving home, geese murdered and terrorists attacking a great city. I'm sure your quilt will provide you with much happier memories.

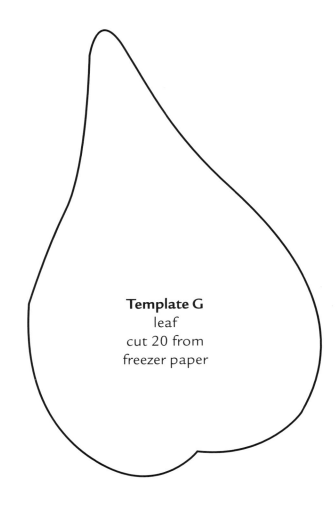

Template G
leaf
cut 20 from
freezer paper

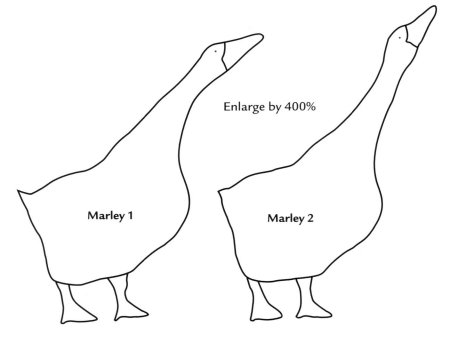

Enlarge by 400%

Marley 1

Marley 2

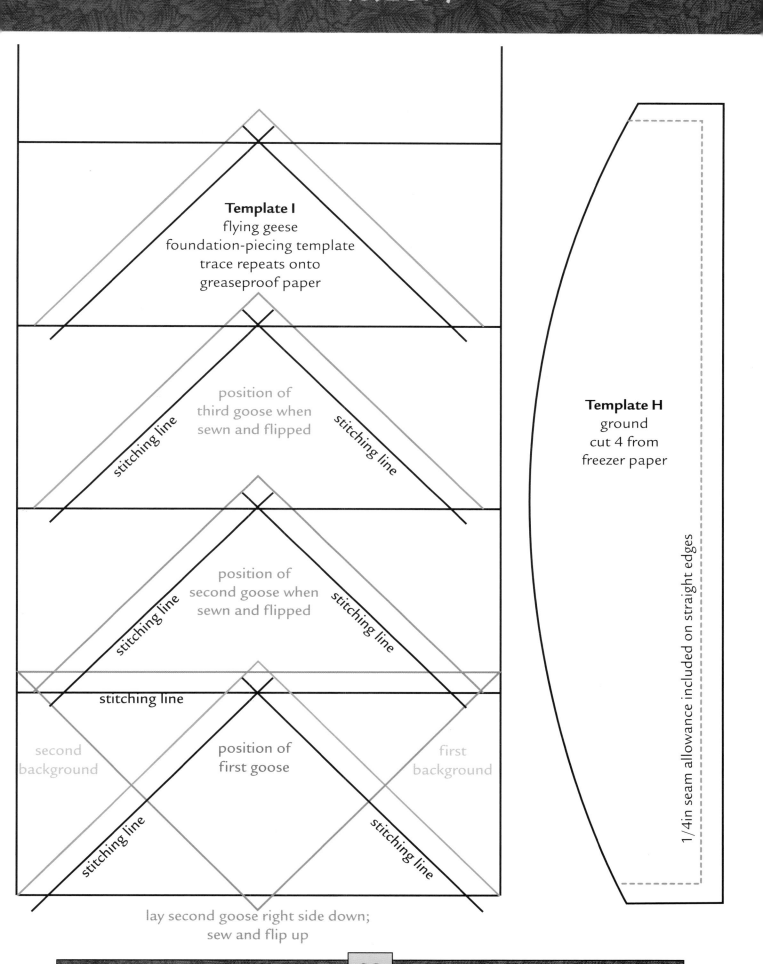

Template I
flying geese
foundation-piecing template
trace repeats onto
greaseproof paper

position of
third goose when
sewn and flipped

stitching line

stitching line

position of
second goose when
sewn and flipped

stitching line

stitching line

stitching line

second
background

position of
first goose

first
background

stitching line

stitching line

lay second goose right side down;
sew and flip up

Template H
ground
cut 4 from
freezer paper

1/4in seam allowance included on straight edges

New York Beauty Blocks

In Book One we used iron-on interfacing to turn under the edges of a Dresden Plate (see page 37) which had many different fabrics along the appliqué edge. Since the New York Beauty also has multicoloured edges, using the interfacing to turn them over is an obvious choice. It has the added benefit of protecting your points and keeping them very sharp almost effortlessly!

If you've looked at this block and thought, 'Oh NO! I **never** could do that!': think again. With **IMA** and foundation-piecing, this block is not only easy, but great fun to make as well. Honestly, I was only going to make a few sample blocks for a foundation-piecing class but once I began, it was like eating popcorn: I just couldn't stop. *Listen to the Leaves Singing* almost made itself! Why not make a spring garden in lovely pastels, or a summer quilt in vibrant, sun-kissed colours? You'll really impress your quilting friends, and I'll help keep your secret on just how easy it was to do ....

Making a New York Beauty block

For each basic New York Beauty block you will need:

- 8in square of neutral background fabric
- 2¼ x 23in strip of light fabric for the inside points
- 2¼ x 23in strip of dark fabric for the outside points
- 5in square of fabric for the large Drunkard's Path curve
- 3in square of fabric for the small Drunkard's Path curve
- 8in square of iron-on interfacing
- freezer paper
- greaseproof paper
- spray starch and brush
- cotton thread in a neutral colour

1 Use templates **B** and **C** to make one large and one small Drunkard's Path curves from freezer paper. Use Method 1 (see page 36) and the large and small squares of fabric to prepare the curved patches (**a**); set these aside.

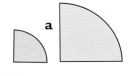

2 Trace a foundation arc (template **A**) onto greaseproof paper using a pencil and a ruler.

Be aware that if you photocopy the arc shape there could be some distortion! Always photocopy from the original: never copy a copy.

3 Thread your machine with the neutral thread and shorten the stitch; the shorter stitch will make the paper removal easier. Place the light and dark strips of fabric right sides together, with the dark strip on top. With the marked side of the paper arc facing you, place the set of strips (dark on top, remember!) under the pattern with the raw edge extending at least ¼in above the right side of the first point (**b**). Hold the unit up to a light to make sure that the right-hand raw edges of the strips extend at least ¼in beyond the drawn line.

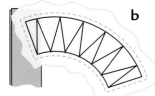

4 Begin stitching two or three stitches from the top edge of the point, and stitch through all three layers, straight down the drawn line to just beyond the curved line at the bottom (**c**). You must stitch exactly on your drawn line to ensure perfect points!

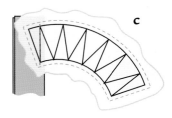

5 Fold the paper to the left along line 1 (**d**). Trim any excess fabric away to within ¼in of the paper's edge. Flatten the paper back out again, flip it over and open the light strip out (**e**); finger press the seam.

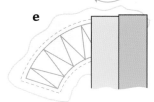

reverse side of foundation   reverse side of foundation

6 Once again flip the unit over so that the paper is on the top and fold the pattern to the left along line 2. Trim to within ¼in of the paper edge; there's a product available to help you do this called Add-A-Quarter – or just use your ruler. Flatten out the paper, flip the unit over and lay the right side of the dark strip along the newly-trimmed edge of the light strip.

7 Hold the two strips firmly in place, flip the unit over and stitch as in steps 4-6. You now have one perfect point (**f**).

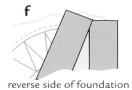

f

reverse side of foundation

8 Continue with this process around the arc shape, alternating light and dark strips until the arc is complete. Trim the excess fabric just *outside* the outer curved line (**g**).

g

9 Press well, but don't remove the paper just yet. Follow the instructions on page 37 to prepare the shape for IMA by using iron-on interfacing; only tear the paper away once you've sewn the 'scary close' seam. Removing the paper takes time, but if your stitches are small enough it shouldn't take too long.

10 Place the arc onto the background square and IMA in place (**h**). Place the prepared large Drunkard's Path curve over the base of the arc and IMA it in place (**i**); cut away the background fabric and remove the freezer paper.

11 Position the smaller Drunkard's Path curve in the corner of the block and IMA it in place (**j**); cut away the fabric from behind the curve and remove the freezer paper. Your New York Beauty block is now complete.

h

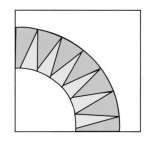

i

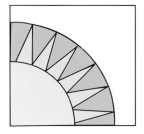

j

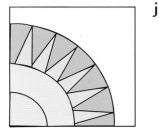

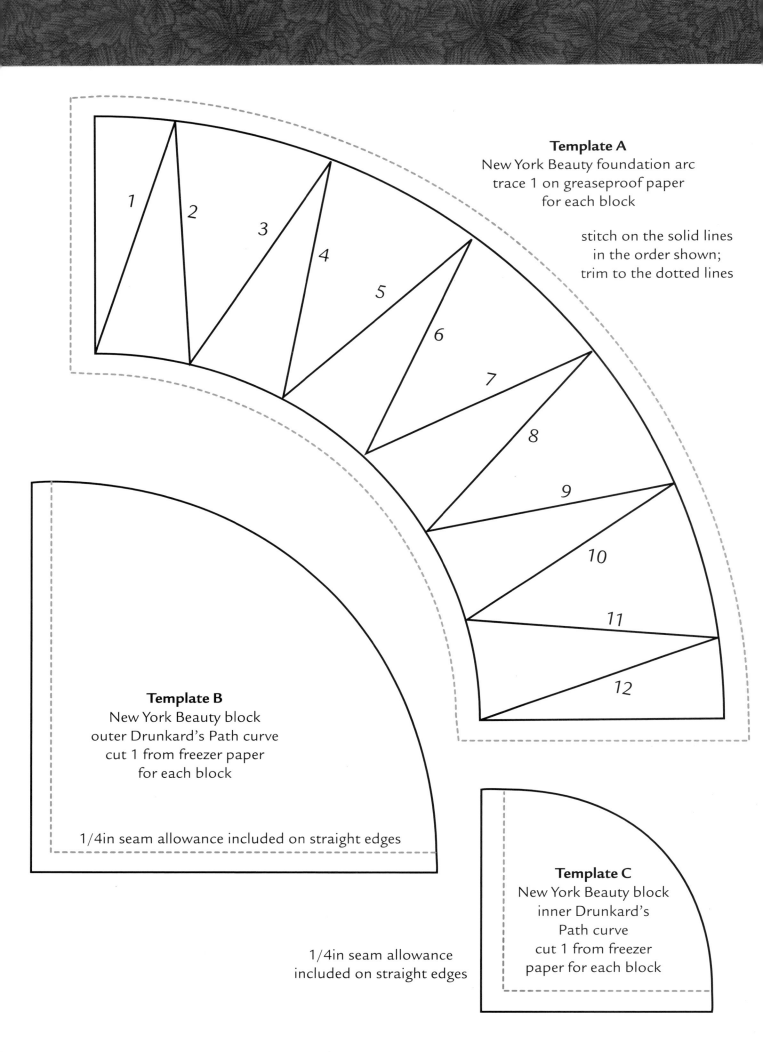

Template A
New York Beauty foundation arc
trace 1 on greaseproof paper
for each block

stitch on the solid lines
in the order shown;
trim to the dotted lines

1 2 3 4 5 6 7 8 9 10 11 12

Template B
New York Beauty block
outer Drunkard's Path curve
cut 1 from freezer paper
for each block

1/4in seam allowance included on straight edges

Template C
New York Beauty block
inner Drunkard's
Path curve
cut 1 from freezer
paper for each block

1/4in seam allowance
included on straight edges

Listen To The Leaves Singing

Green, brown, yellow, orange and red are MY colours, and 32 years of fabric collecting have provided me with an abundance of 'autumn' in my stash! I'd been planning to try using IMA and iron-on interfacing to simplify the New York Beauty block, so I suppose that *Listen To The Leaves Singing* was a quilt just waiting to happen.

As the blocks almost literally flew out of my machine I couldn't help but remember a dry September in 1976; during our annual repatriation to Colorado from Saudi Arabia, where we were living, my family was visiting London. My daughter Hollis (born in Saudi and then only two years old) had never seen deciduous trees. She was most concerned about why all these trees were 'falling apart', but worry turned to delight when I suggested she try skipping through the piles of dry leaves in Green Park. 'Mom!', she shouted over her shoulder as the leaves crunched under her feet; 'Listen; the leaves are singing to me!' Memories like that are not soon forgotten.

TOP: *Here is Hollis (on the left) some 27 years later with her sister Rachel on a nippy autumn day in Scotland. She no longer tries to put the leaves back on trees!*

LEFT: *Grandchildren Mason and Sierra with daughter-in-law Renee join Hollis and her daughter Anastasia amongst the aspens in Colorado last fall.*

In this quilt I will show you how to try another way to appliqué leaves. No bonding web but also no turned edges. The appliqué is done with the quilting! A super opportunity to play with all those lovely threads you have been collecting.

Quilt dimensions: 66in square

You will need:

For the blocks

for the backgrounds:

❖ various tone-on-tone neutral fabrics to equal 2yd, or 36 8in squares

for the New York Beauty arcs and points:

❖ 36 2¼ x 28in strips in various dark autumn prints and batiks, cut into 7 2¼ x 4in pieces

❖ 36 2¼ x 24in strips in various light autumn prints and batiks, cut into 6 2¼ x 4in pieces

for the Drunkard's Path curves:

❖ 36 5in squares of different fabrics for the large curves

❖ 36 3in squares of different fabrics for the small curves

For the leaf border

❖ 4 different strips of fabric each measuring 8 x 60in

❖ 24 6in squares of fat wadding

❖ 24 6in squares of leaf-like fabrics

❖ ½yd total of assorted neutral fabrics for the appliquéd triangles

For the final pieced border

for the backgrounds:

❖ 28 7½ x 5½in rectangles of neutral prints

for the New York Beauty arcs:

❖ 28 2¼ x 23in strips of dark autumn prints and batiks

❖ 28 2¼ x 23in strips of light autumn prints and batiks

for the inner curves:

❖ 28 7 x 2in pieces of different fabrics

for the corner squares:

❖ 4 5½in squares of neutral fabric

❖ 4 3in squares of print fabric

For the binding

❖ cut 8 3½in wide strips and piece to make 320in of binding

Other requirements

❖ 2yd freezer paper

❖ 3yd greaseproof (tracing) paper for foundation piecing

❖ 2yd medium-weight iron-on interfacing

❖ **threads:** YLI Wonder Invisible in clear, Jeans Stitch in brown, various different threads to appli-quilt the leaves, YLI Wash-A-Way thread, 100% cotton thread for piecing (I used grey)

Making the central blocks

1 Rotary-cut 36 8in squares of neutral background fabrics. Cut each square once diagonally (**a**), shuffle the fabrics and then sew the triangles back together in pairs, creating many different combinations (**b**).

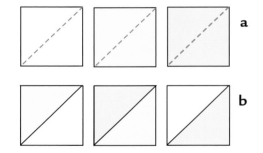

2 Refer back to page 94 for detailed instructions on constructing the New York Beauty blocks. Trace template **A** on page 96 onto the greaseproof paper 36 times, then use these shapes and your New York Beauty arc fabrics to foundation-piece 36 finished arcs. Prepare them with interfacing and IMA one curve onto each pieced background block (**c**), using the diagonal line across the block to help you align the curve evenly.

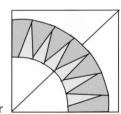

3 Trace templates **B** and **C** on page 96 onto the freezer paper (you'll need 36 of each) and cut the shapes out. Use these shapes and method 1 to prepare 36 large Drunkard's Path curves from the 5in squares of fabric, and 36 small curves from the 3in squares of fabric. IMA these into position on the background blocks (**d**).

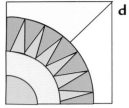

4 Prepare all the blocks in the same way and then sew them together as shown in diagram **e**. The central panel of your quilt is now complete.

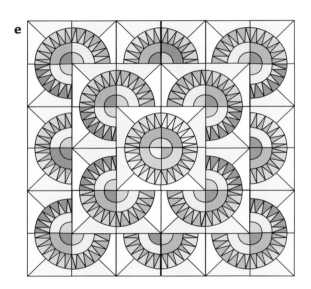

Adding the leaf border

1 Tear four 8 x 60in strips; spray-starch the fabric to give it extra body and press the strips.

2 Cut 12 5¼in squares of various neutral background fabrics and cut them in half diagonally. Cut 12 4½in squares of freezer paper and cut these in half diagonally to create 24 smaller triangles. Use Method 1 to prepare these triangles for IMAing (**f**).

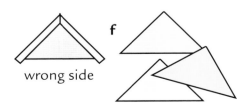
wrong side

3 Position six of these prepared triangles along each border edge, overlapping each triangle edge by ¼in. The base of each triangle should match the arc block that it's going to touch on the central panel (**g**). IMA each triangle in position.

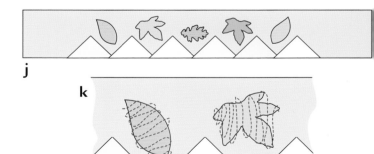

4 Draw around the leaf shapes (templates **D-G**) on freezer paper (you'll need 24 shapes in total); cut the shapes out and press them onto the right sides of your chosen leaf fabric squares (**h**). Cut each leaf shape out (**i**) and remove the freezer paper; you don't need to add any seam allowance.

5 Position five leaves on each border piece (one between each pair of triangles) and pin the shapes in place (**j**). Lower the feed dogs on your machine. Change to a darning foot, and thread with YLI Wash-A-Way; keep cotton in the bobbin. Zigzag freely across each leaf shape to secure it (**k**); try using a 90/14 embroidery needle, and sew slowly.

6 Place a square of fat wadding (polyester is best) behind each leaf. Stitch freely around each leaf just outside the fabric; this secures the wadding. Now cut away the excess wadding; only the leaf is now stuffed (see the sequence of photographs above right).

Step 4   *Step 5*   *Step 6*   *Step 7*   *veins added with Jeans Stitch*

7 Rethread your machine with the thread of your choice; now work free-form quilting all over the leaf, making sure that you go over the edges often enough to secure the fabric in place. I used YLI Jeans Stitch and a 90/14 embroidery needle to free-embroider the stems and veins of the leaves. Work by eye, following the rough pattern on the template; each leaf will be individual … just as in nature!

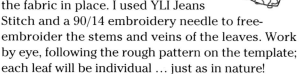

8 Sew the finished border strips onto the body of the quilt, mitre the corners, and appliqué a large leaf at each corner (**I**) – see the detail at the bottom of the page.

I

Adding the outer border

1 The final, outer border is made up of 28 border arcs (7 on each side) which are just slightly different from the ones you've already made. Trace 28 copies of template **H** onto the greaseproof paper; foundation-piece the points as before (**m**).

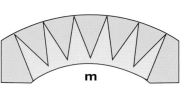

m

2 Trace template **I** onto the freezer paper 28 times and cut out the shapes; use spray starch and the 7 x 2in fabric pieces to prepare 28 inner curve shapes (**n**).

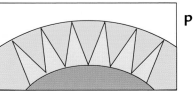

n   *wrong side*

3 IMA each foundation-pieced arc onto a 5½ x 7½in rectangle (**o**). (My rectangles were pieced using two sets of half-square triangles, but I suggest using a single rectangle, which will look just as good and take half the time!) IMA an inner curve onto each block (**p**); cut away the background fabric and remove the freezer paper shapes.

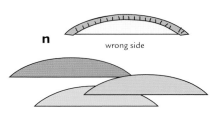

o

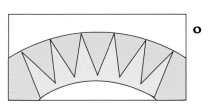

P

q

r

s

t

4 Join the finished arc blocks into strips of seven blocks (**q**). Sew one arc border strip onto the top of the central panel (**r**), and one onto the bottom.

5 Trace four copies of template **C** (page 96) onto freezer paper and cut the shapes out; use these and the four 3in squares of fabric to prepare four small Drunkard's Path curves. IMA each one onto a 5½in corner square (**s**), and sew one square on each end of the remaining seven-arc strips (**t**). Sew these onto the sides of the quilt (**u**).

Finishing

Press the whole quilt top well and prepare it for quilting, layering it with your backing fabric and wadding. I machine quilted the vast majority of the background, but my love of hand quilting got to me in the end and I hand quilted the points (see the diagram below). Follow the instructions on page 20 to bind the edges of the finished quilt.

The Wash-A-Way thread will disappear the first time you wash the quilt. If you can't wait, you can mist it with a plant mister or rub over it with a damp cloth.

u

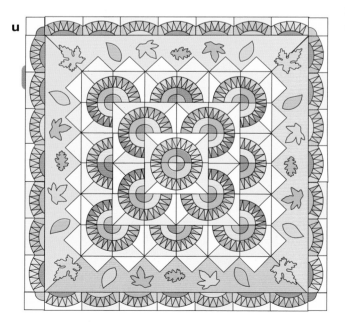

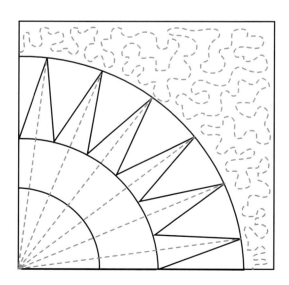

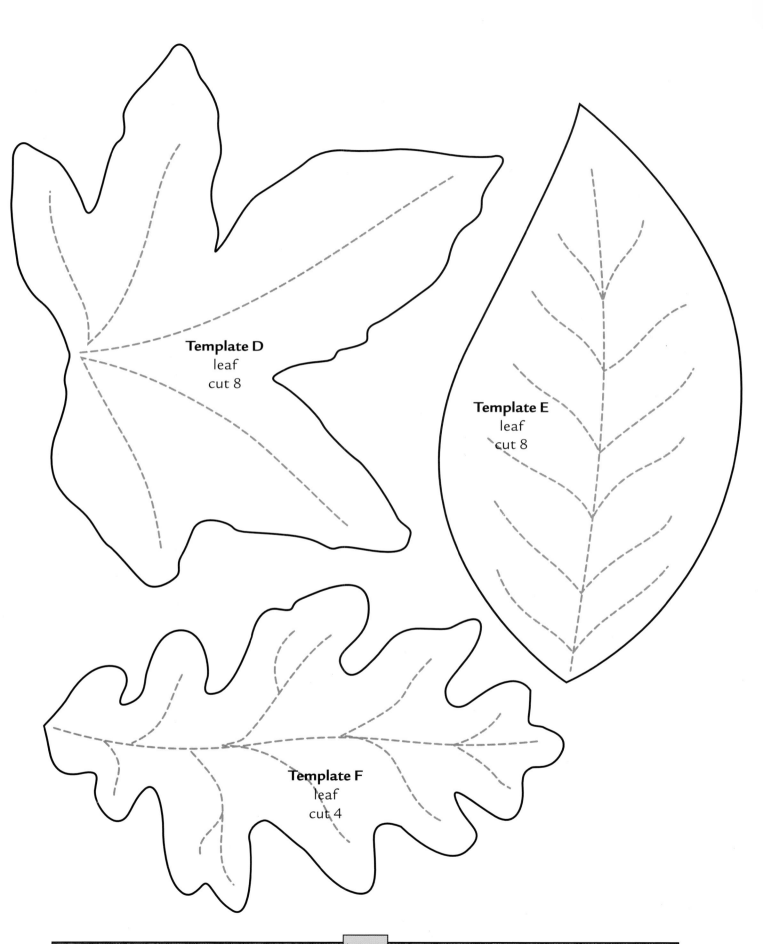

Template D
leaf
cut 8

Template E
leaf
cut 8

Template F
leaf
cut 4

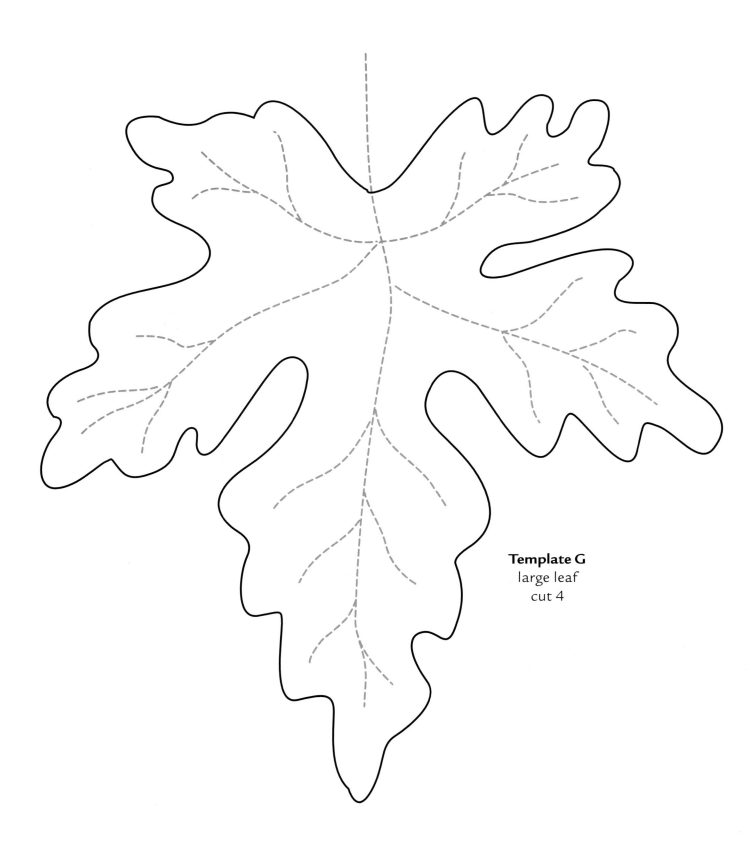

Template G
large leaf
cut 4

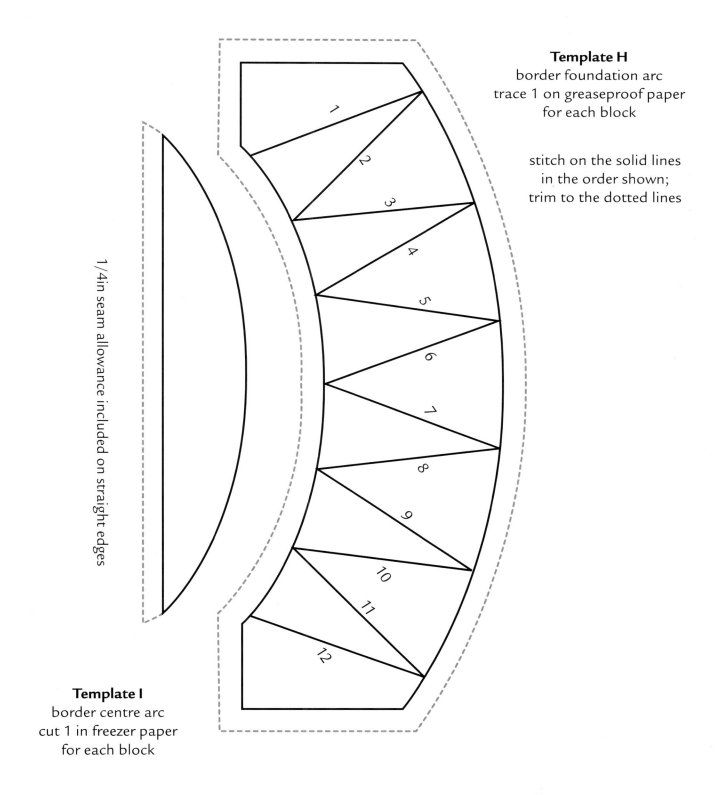

Template H
border foundation arc
trace 1 on greaseproof paper
for each block

stitch on the solid lines
in the order shown;
trim to the dotted lines

1/4in seam allowance included on straight edges

Template I
border centre arc
cut 1 in freezer paper
for each block

Baltimore-Style IMA

a

b

c

d

The timeless beauty of Baltimore-style quilts can be yours with IMA. There are many lovely classic designs available, which you can create in IMA simply by enlarging them. Why fiddle with tiny pieces in a 12in block when you can enlarge it to 24in and make each piece much more do-able! Also, you'll need fewer blocks to finish your quilt ...

In this style of appliqué you'll often be building up your flowers or designs by adding shapes on top of other shapes. Most good appliqué patterns will have a numbered sequence for you to follow as you stitch; remember, stitch as the flower grows – stems, leaves, buds and then flowers. The sequence (**a-d**, above) shows the order for building up a composite design such as the urn of flowers on *Try To Remember* ...

Cut away your background and remove the freezer paper before you add a piece on top of a previously IMAed piece. When shapes overlap you don't need to turn under the bits that are going to be covered, as with the part-leaves under the wavy flower (**e**), and the flower base of the yellow flower (**f**).

e

f

Try To Remember...

Try To Remember ... was my challenge quilt. Based on traditional four-block
appliqué quilts, I designed this quilt just to see if I could do it!
I used both hand appliqué and IMA, and then quilted it at ½in intervals
completely by hand. I absolutely loved every moment of making it.

The nicest compliment I ever received on
Try To Remember ... was from a lovely, elderly
gentleman when the quilt was hung at one of
England's largest quilt shows. I saw him
standing, seemingly forever, just staring. Finally
he turned to me and said, 'Now that's a REAL
quilt. This is the best thing here.' He smiled and
walked away, leaving me speechless!

Sandi Lush, probably England's finest hand
quilter, has been strongly suggesting for years
that I really should leave this quilt to her in my
will. Hang in there, Sandi, you never know ...

So, if this quilt has taken hold of you as well,
why not make it!? Yes, it may well be your
challenge quilt too but remember 'Nothing
great was ever achieved without enthusiasm'
(Ralph Waldo Emerson), and I'm sure you
have heaps of that!

If you can't face a full-size quilt, why not make
one block as a cushion cover or small wall
hanging?

Quilt dimensions: 77in square

You will need:

For the background, border and binding
❖ 6yd

For the appliqué and embellishment
❖ ¾yd medium rust fabric
❖ 2yd dark rust fabric
❖ ½yd gold fabric
❖ ¼yd variegated gold fabric
❖ 3½yd green fabric
❖ ¼yd variegated green fabric
❖ scraps of yellow fabric
❖ gold silk embroidery thread to embellish
  flowers, and brown for the fruit stems

For the backing
❖ 5yd

Other requirements
❖ 77in square wadding (as this was totally hand
  quilted I used Mountain Mist Quilt-Light
  wadding)
❖ 3yd freezer paper
❖ greaseproof paper
❖ ½yd lightweight iron-on interfacing
❖ template plastic
❖ **threads:** YLI Hand Quilting thread and
  Wonder Invisible thread, 100% cotton thread
  – 50/3 for piecing, 60/2 ply for bobbin under
  the Invisible
❖ spray starch and brush

You'll be using the various fabrics to make the following parts of the design:

background fabric:
- 4 25½in squares
- 4 13½ x 76½in strips for the border
- 8 3½ x 42in strips for the binding

medium rust fabric:
- 48 2½ x 1½in strips for pieced flowers (template E3)
- 20 spiky flowers (template B)
- 20 Suffolk Puffs/yoyos (template G)

dark rust fabric:
- 4 patches for pieced flowers (template E1)
- 48 2½ x 1½in strips for pieced flowers (template E4)
- 4 tree pots (template H)
- 32 rosebuds (template F)
- 24 wavy flowers (template A1)
- 12 apples (template I)

gold fabric:
- 16 patches for pieced flowers (template E2)
- 4 half-flowers (template C)

- 8 birds (template J)
- 8 bird wings (template K)

variegated gold fabric:
- 12 pears (template L)

green fabric:
- 4 flower-bases (template D)
- 120 part-leaves (template A2)
- 112 large leaves (template M)
- 76 small leaves (template N)
- 16 oak leaves (template O)
- 32 calyxes (template P)
- 4 trees (template Q)
- 17yd bias binding

variegated green fabric:
- 4 flower urns (template R)

Preparation

1 Trace all the pieces A-R onto the template plastic and cut them out to create templates. For shapes A-D and I-R inclusive, and shapes E1 and E2, you need to cut a series of freezer paper shapes; trace the necessary number of each shape onto the freezer paper, and cut all the shapes out.

 **You might find it helpful to use several small, clear re-sealable bags to keep your freezer paper shapes together in batches.**

2 From the green fabric cut 1in-wide strips of bias and make up 17yd of bias stems (½in finished width).

3 From the background fabric, cut or tear:
- four 13½ x 76½in strips (marked ■)
- four 25½in squares (marked •)
- eight 3½ x 40in strips for the binding (marked ı)

	spare		■		■
					■
	•	•	•	•	■

Making the rosebuds and simple flowers

1 To create the rosebuds, use template F to cut 32 circles from the dark rust fabric. Fold each one in half (**a**), wrong sides together, then fold both bottom corners into the centre (**b**). Use the hand quilting thread to sew a long running stitch about a quarter of the way up from the bottom (**c**); be sure to make a big knot at the end, because now you're going to pull the thread up tight to gather the rosebud (while ye may!), as shown in **d**.

a   b   c   d

2 To make the wavy flowers: use Method 1 (see page 36) to prepare 24 flower shapes, using the freezer paper shapes you've cut from template A1, and the dark rust fabric (**e**). Prepare 120 part-leaf shapes using the freezer paper shapes you've cut from template A2, and the green fabric (**f**). Only fold the fabric over the edges of the leaf shapes; the bases will be covered by the edges of the wavy flower once you've IMAed them both to the quilt top (**g**).

 e   f

g

3 To make the spiky flowers: use Method 1 to prepare 20 flower shapes, using the freezer paper shapes you've cut from template B, and the medium rust fabric (**h**). Use template G to cut 20 circles from the medium rust fabric, and follow the instructions on page 72 to make them into Suffolk Puffs/yoyos, taking a scant ¼in seam allowance (**i**). (Again it's best to use the quilting thread for this job.) You'll appliqué one yoyo flower centre onto the right side of each flower once the flower is IMAed to the quilt top (**j**).

h i

j

4 To make the half-flowers: use Method 1 to prepare four half-flower shapes, using the freezer paper shapes you've cut from template C, and the gold fabric (**k**). Prepare four flower bases in the same way, using the freezer paper shapes you've cut from template D, and the green fabric (**l**), but leave the top curved edge unturned. IMA the bottom of each half flower shape over the unturned edge of a flower base (**m**).

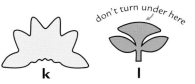

don't turn under here

k   l

m

Making the pieced flowers

1 Trace the pointed shape E3/E4 four times onto greaseproof paper and follow the instructions on page 95 to foundation-piece the design using the medium rust fabric for the inside points and the dark rust for the outside points (**n**).

I found it best to do each circle of foundation-piecing in two halves, then sew them together. Cut along the dotted line marked, and piece the points and part-points all round each semi-circle; when all the pieces are in position, lay the semicircles right sides together and join them.

2 Cut a 3½in circle of dark rust fabric and set aside. Iron four E2 freezer paper templates onto the gold fabric and press under only one edge. Place these on the dark rust circle (**o**) and IMA the turned edge of each shape. Iron on the E1 freezer paper circle and turn under both the gold and the rust fabric edges. Place the shape over the pieced circle and IMA in place (**p**). Cut away the dark rust fabric and remove the freezer paper. Then use iron-on interfacing to turn over the outside pointed edges of each flower (see page 37).

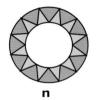 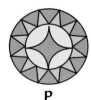

n   **o**   **p**

Appliquéing the blocks

1 Fold each square of background fabric in half diagonally in both directions and press in the folds; IMA bias stems in the positions shown (**q**), using the creases to help you place them evenly. (Appliqué the stems right across the centre of the square, to help keep them even; you'll then put the central flower over them.)

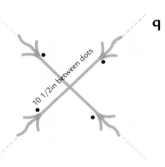

q

10 1/2in between dots

2 The oak leaves on my quilt were appliquéd by hand, as pressing all those tiny dips under was too daunting. If you don't want to appliqué by hand, I suggest that you simplify the shape – as shown by the dotted line around the template – for easier IMAing. I don't believe that this will compromise the final look at all! Prepare the leaf shapes according to whichever method you're using, and appliqué four onto each block as shown (**r**).

r

3 Position a pieced flower over the bases of the oak leaves and stems on each block and IMA in place (**s**). IMA the remaining flowers and leaves in the positions shown (**t**); you'll use four buds and calyxes, eight large leaves, four small ones, four wavy flowers and their leaves, and four spiky flowers on each block. If you wish, embroider the wavy flowers using the silk thread after they've been appliquéd; I used two rows of chain stitch for the curves and put a wrapped spider's web in the centre. (These are created by stitching eight spikes and then weaving the thread over and under the spikes until the web is complete, as shown *right*.)

s

t

Making the quilt top

1 Press and trim each finished block to 24½in square. Sew the four blocks together, press well and measure the pieced panel for your borders. I've allowed a few extra inches on the border lengths so that you can custom-fit them and mitre them successfully. I found that folding the border strips into four and pressing them before I stitched them onto the sides gave me a reliable guide for placement of the appliquéd pieces.

u

2 Prepare four flower urns with spray starch using the freezer paper shapes you've cut from template R and the variegated green fabric. Appliqué the meandering leaf-and-rosebud stems and the central design along each border piece as shown (**u**); finish the end of each stem roughly 12in in from the unmitred edge of the border strip so that you leave room for the corner trees. Sew the borders on and mitre the corners with IMA.

3 Prepare the shapes for the trees, tree pots, birds (and wings), apples and pears with spray starch, then IMA them over the mitred corners (**v**). Add little embroidered stems for the fruit, using the brown embroidery thread, and embroider the birds' feet.

Quilting and finishing

I love hand quilting and so wanted to do lots of it. The appliqué design on this quilt was very strong, though, and I didn't want to 'gild the lily' with too much fancy quilting. I was resigned to doing a simple diagonal line all across the surface until my mom pointed out that the straight lines would be too harsh with the gentle curves of the appliqué – so why didn't I just make 'curvy lines'? Why not indeed! I decided to do the curves at 45° across each quarter of the quilt (**w**), with the lines meeting at a 90° angle down the centre lines of the quilt.

v

ABOVE: *centre quilting design*
BELOW: *pieced flower*

It took days of designing and planning to figure out how to guarantee that the curve would go under a leaf or flower and come out at the other end correctly so that it would match the curves coming from the other direction! My solution was my plastic 'worm' (see template S). I found that by adding guide bars at the top and base of each curve I could use them as registration lines. I marked one curve, top and bottom, then went back and made a small dot at the top and base of each line. Then when I moved the worm down to mark the next line I made sure every line touched each dot (now at the top of the worm). It made all the difference! The quilted flower design in the centre of the quilt (template T) eliminates the need to make all the curves match when they meet. Still I had to send the family off on a cheap day-trip to France so that I could have 100% peace and quiet for the 12 hours it took to mark the top. I couldn't stand straight for days, but I knew the quilting would be perfect.

Don't you just hate it when Mom is right? No, really: Mom's suggestion was the maraschino cherry on the quilting cake. I loved every moment of quilting *Try To Remember ...*, and truly felt sad when it was done.

So, use my worm to mark your quilt top, or mark it for quilting in any other design that you fancy. Layer your backing, wadding and quilt top, then quilt by hand or machine. Piece together your 3½in binding strips, and follow the instructions on page 20 to bind your quilt.

'Life is either a daring adventure, or nothing.'

Helen Keller

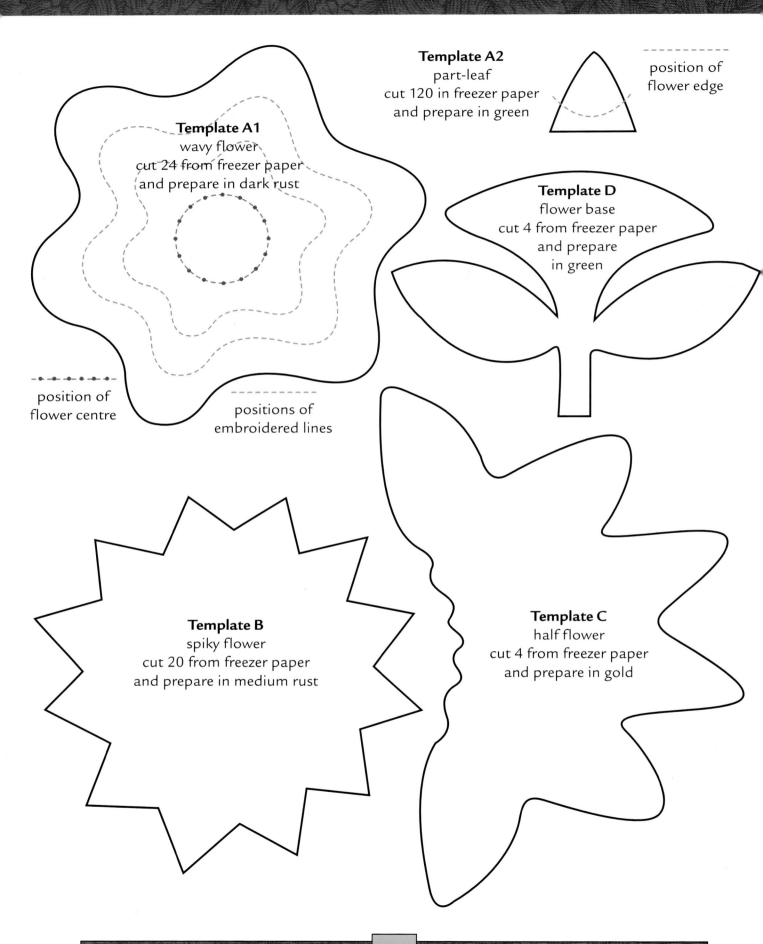

Template A1
wavy flower
cut 24 from freezer paper
and prepare in dark rust

Template A2
part-leaf
cut 120 in freezer paper
and prepare in green

position of
flower edge

Template D
flower base
cut 4 from freezer paper
and prepare
in green

position of
flower centre

positions of
embroidered lines

Template B
spiky flower
cut 20 from freezer paper
and prepare in medium rust

Template C
half flower
cut 4 from freezer paper
and prepare in gold

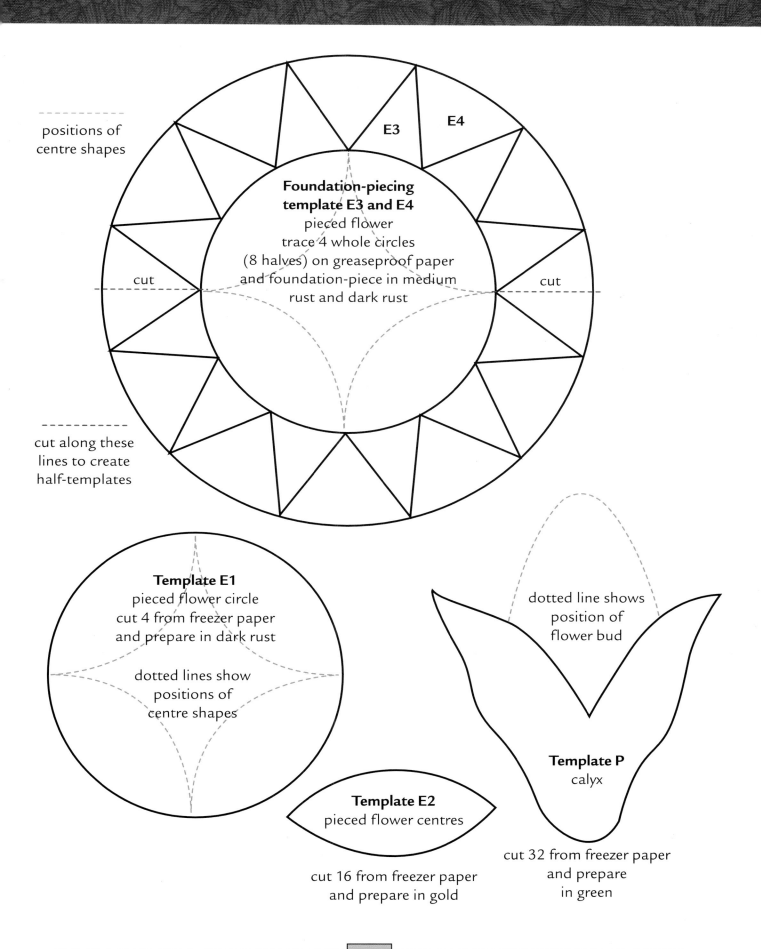

positions of
centre shapes

E3

E4

**Foundation-piecing
template E3 and E4**
pieced flower
trace 4 whole circles
(8 halves) on greaseproof paper
and foundation-piece in medium
rust and dark rust

cut

cut

cut along these
lines to create
half-templates

Template E1
pieced flower circle
cut 4 from freezer paper
and prepare in dark rust

dotted lines show
positions of
centre shapes

dotted line shows
position of
flower bud

Template P
calyx

cut 32 from freezer paper
and prepare
in green

Template E2
pieced flower centres

cut 16 from freezer paper
and prepare in gold

Template F
rosebud

cut 32 in dark rust

Template G
Suffolk Puff/yoyo

cut 20 in medium rust

Template O
oak leaf
cut 16 from freezer paper
and prepare in green

solid line shows
cutting line for
hand appliqué shapes

dotted line shows
cutting line for
IMA shapes

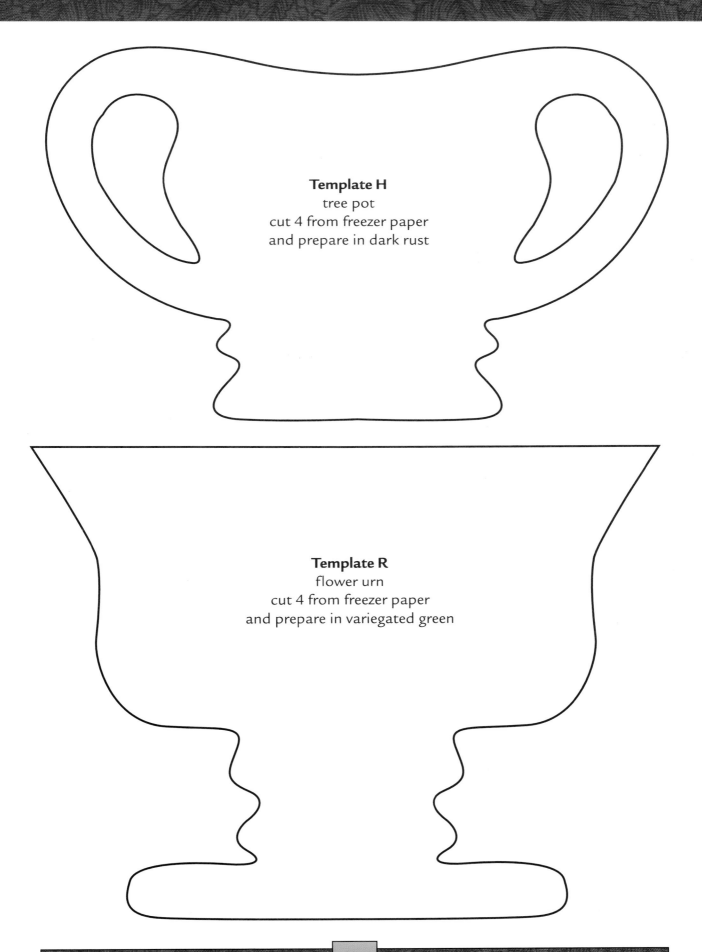

Template H
tree pot
cut 4 from freezer paper
and prepare in dark rust

Template R
flower urn
cut 4 from freezer paper
and prepare in variegated green

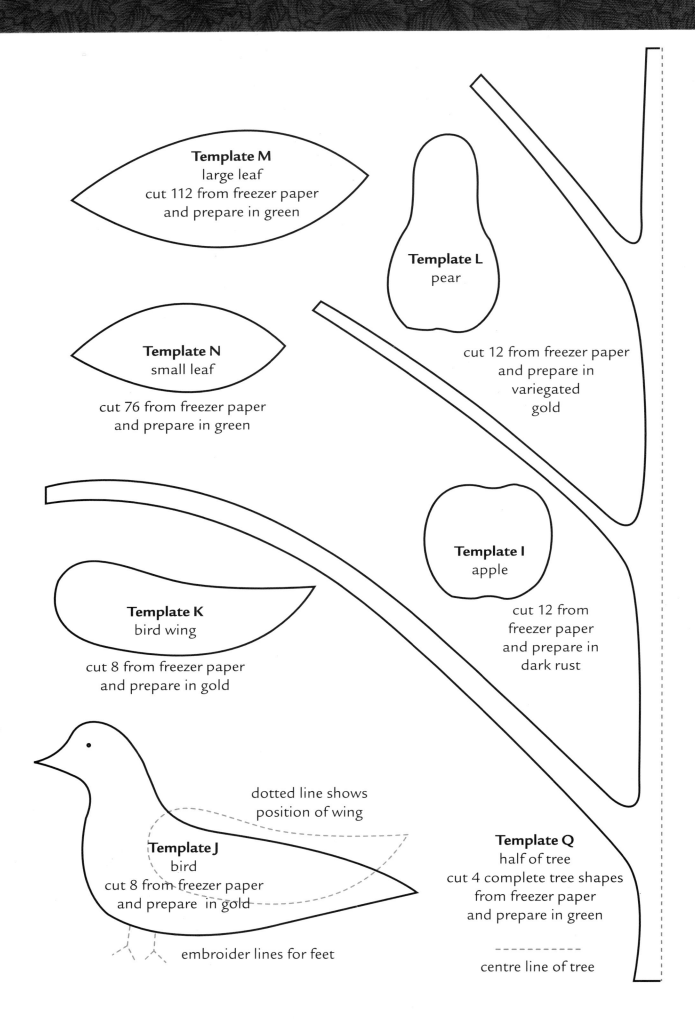

Template M
large leaf
cut 112 from freezer paper
and prepare in green

Template L
pear

cut 12 from freezer paper
and prepare in
variegated
gold

Template N
small leaf

cut 76 from freezer paper
and prepare in green

Template I
apple

cut 12 from
freezer paper
and prepare in
dark rust

Template K
bird wing

cut 8 from freezer paper
and prepare in gold

dotted line shows
position of wing

Template J
bird
cut 8 from freezer paper
and prepare in gold

Template Q
half of tree
cut 4 complete tree shapes
from freezer paper
and prepare in green

- - - - - - - - - -
centre line of tree

embroider lines for feet

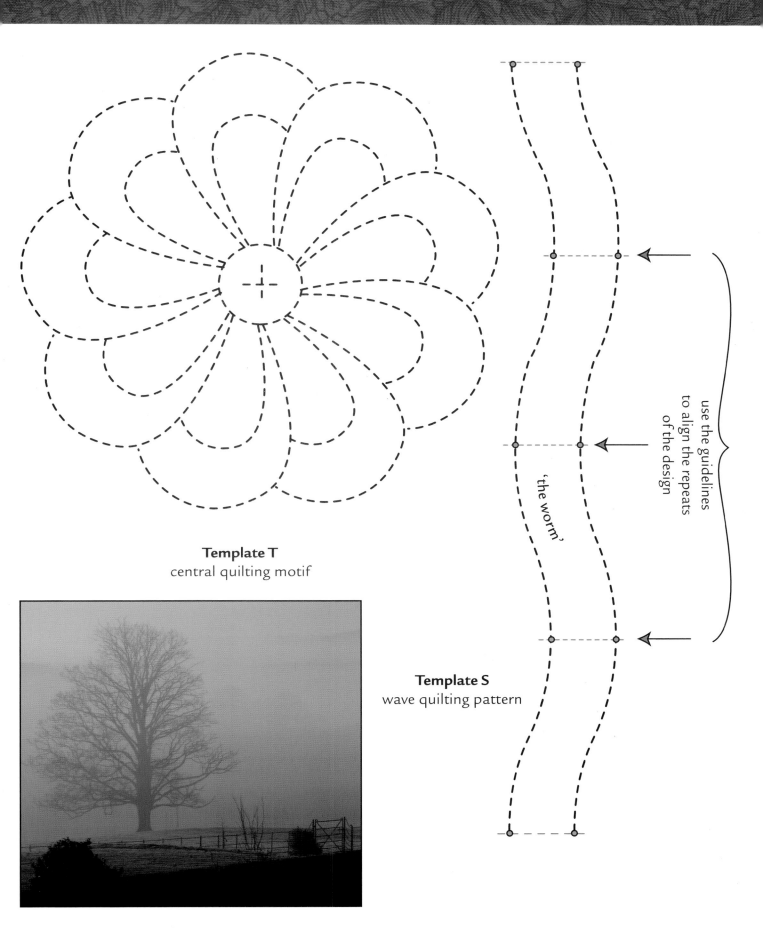

Template T
central quilting motif

use the guidelines
to align the repeats
of the design

'the worm'

Template S
wave quilting pattern

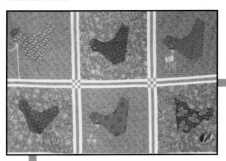

Maureen Blake

Joyce Adams

Kirsty and Una Rawson

Resources and Acknowledgements

• Products mentioned in this book can be found in any good quilt shop, but If you cannot locate a specific item in the UK you could try the mail order company: QUILT DIRECT (free-phone 0500 418 083) www.quiltdirect.com

• Invaluable information on sewing machines came from the very helpful and knowledgeable people at:
World of Sewing, Tunbridge Wells, Kent (01892 536 314)
Sew ... Northampton, Northampton (01604 637 200)

– Machine quilting on *Sheep On My Hills* by Jan Chandler, Quilting Solutions, Bury St Edmunds, Suffolk (01449 736 280)

– *Fairy Frost* was long-arm machine quilted by The Bramble Patch, West Street, Weedon, Northampton NN7 4QU

– *Nana's Butterflies* was photographed at Floral Craft, 8a-10 Church Street, Market Harborough

– *Phoenix Rising* was photographed at Croft Wingates Gallery, 44a St Mary's Road, Market Harborough

– *Find My Friend* was shot in the toy section of Minerva, a lovely gift shop at 2 Stockerston Road, Uppingham, Rutland LE15 9UD

– Aldwinkles Coffee Shop (tucked away behind Floral Craft!) at 8c Church Street, Market Harborough, Leics LE16 7AA was the location for *Trees Please* (Blocking Your Quilt chapter)

Geese in the Garden was photographed at Farndon Fields Farm Shop, Market Harborough, courtesy of Milly (01858 464 838)

– *Sheep On My Hills* was photographed at Foxton Locks, Leicestershire

• The majority of photos provided by
Steve Sullivan, 3 Harecombe Road, Crowborough, East Sussex TN6 1NE
(01892 654 309) www.sullivanphotos.co.uk
professional photography with a personal touch

• Wholesale Distributors for *Invisible Machine Appliqué* and *Invisible Machine Appliqué and Beyond*:

UK:
EQS, 11 Iliffe House, Iliffe Ave, Oadby, Leicester LE2 5LS
EQS, a wholesale company, kindly supplied some of the waddings, YLI threads, notions and fabrics for the photography in this book. *Free Spirit* and *Michael Miller* fabrics were used for the page headings and the cover of *Invisible Machine Appliqué and Beyond*.

USA and AUSTRALIA:
Quilters' Resource, PO Box 148850, Chicago 60614 Ill USA (001 773 278 5695)

AND A SPECIAL THANK YOU TO:

My son Christopher Scoggin and his wife Renee, who created and continue to maintain my website (www.morningstarquilts.com), and special appreciation to Christopher who unfailingly supports me and ever-so-patiently leads me by the hand through the computer world maze.

• **All quilts in this book are made by Dawn Cameron-Dick unless otherwise noted.** Information on workshops and lectures can be found on my website: www.morningstarquilts.com
or e-mail me at IMA_dawn@hotmail.com

The border on this page is made solely of students' work, so a special thanks goes out to them.

Maureen Kennedy

Jean Hamilton

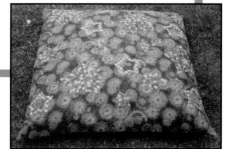

Rebecca Preen